W9-BKB-525

HEALTHY
EATING

A Guide to Nutrition

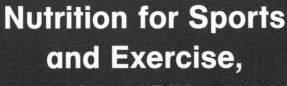

Nutrition for Sports
and Exercise,

Second Edition

HEALTHY EATING: A GUIDE TO NUTRITION

HEALTHY EATING

A Guide to Nutrition

Nutrition for Sports and Exercise,
Second Edition

Lori A. Smolin, Ph.D., and
Mary B. Grosvenor, M.S., R.D.

CHELSEA HOUSE
PUBLISHERS
An imprint of Infobase Publishing

Chelsea House
An imprint of Infobase Publishing
132 West 31st Street
New York, NY 10001

Library of Congress Cataloging-in-Publication Data
Smolin, Lori A.
  Nutrition for sports and exercise / Lori A. Smolin and Mary B. Grosvenor. — 2nd ed.
      p. cm. — (Healthy eating: a guide to nutrition)
  Includes bibliographical references and index.
  ISBN 978-1-60413-804-7 (hardcover)
 1. Nutrition—Popular works. 2. Athletes—Nutrition—Popular works.
3. Exercise—Physiological aspects—Popular works. I. Grosvenor, Mary B. II. Title. III. Series.

  RA784.S598 2010
  613.7—dc22   2010005692

Chelsea House books are available at special discounts when purchased in bulk quantities for businesses, associations, institutions, or sales promotions. Please call our Special Sales Department in New York at (212) 967-8800 or (800) 322-8755.

You can find Chelsea House on the World Wide Web at
http://www.chelseahouse.com

Text design by Annie O'Donnell
Cover design by Alicia Post
Illustrations by Sholto Ainslie for Infobase Publishing
Composition by Mary Susan Ryan-Flynn
Cover printed by Bang Printing, Brainerd, Minn.
Book printed and bound by Bang Printing, Brainerd, Minn.
Date printed: September 2010
Printed in the United States of America

10 9 8 7 6 5 4 3 2 1

This book is printed on acid-free paper.

All links and Web addresses were checked and verified to be correct at the time of publication. Because of the dynamic nature of the Web, some addresses and links may have changed since publication and may no longer be valid.

CONTENTS

INTRODUCTION

A hundred years ago, people received nutritional guidance from mothers and grandmothers: Eat your carrots because they're good for your eyes; don't eat too many potatoes because they'll make you fat; be sure to get plenty of roughage so you can more easily move your bowels. Today, everyone seems to offer more advice: Take a vitamin supplement to optimize your health; don't eat fish with cabbage because you won't be able to digest them together; you can't stay healthy on a vegetarian diet. Nutrition is one of those topics about which all people seem to think they know something, or at least have an opinion. Whether it is the clerk in your local health food store recommending that you buy supplements or the woman behind you in line at the grocery store raving about the latest low-carbohydrate diet, everyone is ready to offer you nutritional advice. How do you know what to believe or, more importantly, what to do?

The purpose of these books is to help you answer these questions. Even if you don't love learning about science, at the very least you probably enjoy certain foods and want to stay healthy—or become healthier. In response to this, these books are designed to make the science you *need* to understand as palatable as the foods you love. Once you understand the basics, you can apply this simple health knowledge to your everyday decisions about nutrition and health. The **Healthy Eating** set includes one book with all of the basic nutrition information you need to choose a healthy diet, as well as five others that cover topics of special concern to many: weight management, exercise, disease prevention, food safety, and eating disorders.

Our goal is not to tell you to stop eating potato chips and candy bars, give up fast food, or always eat your vegetables. Instead, it is to provide you with the information you need to make informed choices about your diet. We hope you will recognize that potato chips and candy are not poison, but they should only be eaten as occasional treats. We hope you will decide for yourself that fast food is something you can indulge in every now and then, but is not a good choice every day. We encourage you to recognize that although you should eat your vegetables, not everyone always does, so you should do your best to try new vegetables and fruits and eat them as often as possible.

These books take the science of nutrition out of the classroom and allow you to apply this information to the choices you make about foods, exercise, dietary supplements, and other lifestyle decisions that are important to your health. This knowledge should help you choose a healthy diet while allowing you to enjoy the diversity of flavors, textures, and tastes that food provides, and also encouraging you to explore the meanings food holds in our society. When you eat a healthy diet, you will feel good in the short term and enjoy health benefits in the long term. We can't personally evaluate each meal you consume, but we believe these books will give you the tools to make your own nutritious choices.

Lori A. Smolin, Ph.D., and
Mary B. Grosvenor, M.S., R.D.

1

NUTRITION, FITNESS, AND HEALTH

What people eat and how active they are determine not only how healthy they are, but also their ability to perform in athletics. It helps to think about the body as a machine. It requires fuel to operate, and it requires proper tuning to operate optimally. The energy and nutrients in food provide fuel for the "human machine" to operate, and physical fitness provides the fine tuning.

WHAT IS A HEALTHY LIFESTYLE?

A healthy lifestyle allows the body to perform at its best. This involves:

- Consuming a healthy diet that prevents nutrient deficiencies and excesses and provides the right number of calories to keep weight in the healthy range

- Participating in the right amount and kinds of physical activity
- Limiting exposure to tobacco, alcohol, and illicit drugs

A healthy lifestyle can keep people fit, energetic, and lean. It also can reduce the chances of developing chronic diseases over time. Learning to choose foods wisely and incorporating exercise into a daily routine can help people live long, healthy lives.

WHAT IS A HEALTHY DIET?

Whether a person is a couch potato or an Olympic hopeful, a healthy diet keeps his or her weight in a desirable range and provides the right combination of **nutrients**:

- The proper balance of carbohydrates, proteins, and fats
- Plenty of water
- Enough (but not too much) essential vitamins and minerals

In general, a healthy diet is rich in whole grains, fruits, and vegetables. It contains the right types of fats and is low in added sugars.

People don't have to give up their favorite foods to eat a healthy diet. No single food or dietary component can make or break a diet. Rather, it is the overall pattern of intake that determines the healthfulness of a diet. Variety is important, because different foods provide different nutrients. For example, strawberries provide vitamin C but little vitamin A. Apricots are a good a source of vitamin A, but provide less vitamin C.

Balance also is part of a healthy diet. Balancing your diet means selecting foods that complement each other. This requires considering the **nutrient density** of the foods you choose. Foods low in nutrient density—such as baked goods, snack foods, and sodas—should be balanced with nutrient-dense choices, such as salads, fruit, vegetables, and low-fat dairy products. If one meal is a burger, fries, and a soda, this can be balanced with a salad, brown rice, and chicken at the next meal.

By eating a varied diet that balances nutrient-poor choices with nutrient-dense ones and is moderate in added sugar and fat, most people can meet their nutrient needs. For people with increased needs or limited food choices, fortified foods are available. These have added nutrients. They include calcium-fortified orange juice and iron-fortified breakfast cereals. In some cases, vitamin and mineral supplements can be helpful, but these should be used with caution to avoid consuming too much of a vitamin or mineral.

DO THE DIETS OF AMERICAN CHILDREN MAKE THE GRADE?

A healthy diet should be based on whole grains, vegetables, and fruits, with smaller amounts of low-fat dairy products, lean meats, and beans. It should include limited amounts of solid fats and added sugar. How do the diets of American children stack up to these recommendations? This question can be answered by scoring their diets using the Healthy Eating Index. This tool evaluates diets based on how well they conform to 12 components of the recommendations of the Dietary Guidelines and MyPyramid. A diet that meets all 12 recommendations would have a score of 100.

The component of children's diets that received the lowest scores, only 0.6 out of 5 possible points, was consumption of dark green and orange vegetables and legumes. Total vegetable consumption was only about half the recommended amount. Total grain consumption met recommendations and received a full score of 5 out of 5, but the amounts of whole grains were far below recommendations and received a score of 0.8 out of 5. The diets also received low scores for intake of saturated fat, sodium, and extra calories from solid fats and added sugars, which were all consumed in excess. Diet quality was poor for all age groups and the combined score for children ages 2 to 17 years old was only 55.9 out of 100. By all accounts, a failing grade.

WHAT IS PHYSICAL FITNESS?

Physical fitness helps people look and feel their best. Fit people can perform physical activity for a longer period than unfit people can. Being fit also reduces the risk of developing chronic diseases such as diabetes, heart disease, and cancer. For athletes, fitness means being able to perform in their sport at their full potential. Fitness level depends on endurance, strength, flexibility, and body composition.

Cardiovascular and Respiratory Endurance

Endurance determines how long a person can jog or ride a bike before becoming exhausted. It is determined by the ability of the heart and lungs to deliver oxygen and nutrients to tissues and remove wastes. Endurance can be enhanced by regular **aerobic exercise**, such as jogging, bicycling, and swimming. To be considered aerobic, an activity must be performed at an intensity that is low enough for a person to carry on a conversation, but high enough that the person cannot sing while exercising.

Regular aerobic exercise strengthens the heart muscle and increases the amount of blood pumped with each heartbeat. This decreases **resting heart rate**, which is the rate at which the heart beats when the body is at rest. The more fit a person is, the lower his or her resting heart rate will be, and the more blood the heart can pump to the muscles during exercise. In addition to increasing the amount of oxygen-rich blood that is pumped to muscles, regular aerobic exercise increases the amount of oxygen the muscles are able to use to provide energy.

Muscle Strength and Endurance

Greater muscle strength enhances the ability to perform tasks such as pushing or lifting. In daily life, this could mean lifting a gallon of milk off the top shelf of the refrigerator with one hand, moving a couch into an apartment, or lifting heavier weights at the gym. Greater muscle endurance allows people to stack wood, shovel snow, or rake leaves for longer periods without getting tired. People improve muscle strength and endurance by using

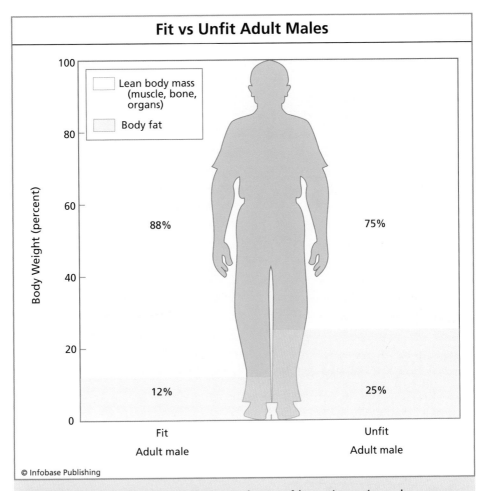

FIGURE 1.1 The human body is made up of lean tissue (muscle, organs, and bone) and fat tissue. The percentage of fat tissue increases without proper nutrition and exercise.

their muscles to move against a resisting force. Weight lifting and other resistance exercises stress the muscles, causing them to increase in size and strength.

Flexibility

Flexibility determines how far muscles and ligaments can be stretched. Regularly moving the arms, legs, neck, and torso through their full range of motion helps increase and maintain flexibility. If flexibility is poor, simple tasks, such as tying shoes or lifting packages from the car, can be difficult. Improving flexibility makes everyday life easier. It also may improve athletic performance and reduce the risk of injuries.

Body Composition

Exercise builds and maintains muscle, so people who are physically fit have a greater proportion of muscle and a smaller proportion of fat than do unfit individuals of the same weight (Figure 1.1). The amount of body fat a person has is affected by gender and age. In general, women have more stored body fat than men, and older adults have more body fat and less muscle than younger adults. A healthy amount of body fat for young adult women is 21% to 32% of total weight; in young adult men, it is 8% to 19%.

THE BENEFITS OF EXERCISE AND A HEALTHY DIET

Heart disease, stroke, cancer, and diabetes are among the leading causes of death in the United States today. They account for about two-thirds of all deaths each year. All of these diseases are related to diet and lifestyle.

A person's genetic makeup is an important determinant of his or her risk for developing these diseases, but lifestyle choices—such as a poor diet, lack of exercise, smoking, and alcohol abuse—also play a vital role. People cannot control the genes they inherit, but they can control the foods they eat and how much exercise they get. A healthy lifestyle can reduce the risk of developing disease, and may slow the progression of any conditions people already have.

A regular program of exercise increases fitness level and helps keep weight within the healthy range. It also reduces the risk of chronic diseases, including heart disease, high blood pressure, stroke, diabetes, cancer, and osteoporosis. In addition, exercise promotes psychological well-being, reduces depression and anxiety, and improves mood, sleep patterns, and overall outlook on life. It stimulates the release of chemicals called **endorphins,** which are thought to be natural tranquilizers that play a role in triggering what athletes describe as an "exercise high." In addition to causing exercise euphoria, endorphins are believed to reduce anxiety, aid in relaxation, and improve mood, pain tolerance, and appetite control.

A Healthy Body Weight

A healthy body weight is associated with well-being and longevity. Carrying excess body fat increases the risks of heart disease, diabetes, stroke, gallbladder disease, sleep disorders, respiratory problems, and some types of cancer. Maintaining weight at a proper level reduces the risks of these diseases. For athletes, a healthy weight can also optimize performance. A calculation of **body mass index (BMI)** can be used to determine if weight is in the healthy range (Figure 1.2). Because BMI considers total body weight, rather than the amount of body weight that is from muscle versus fat, athletes who have a large amount of muscle mass may have a BMI in the overweight or obese range. This does not mean their weight creates a health risk. Only excess weight from fat is considered unhealthy.

Diet and exercise are both essential for maintaining weight. When people consume the same number of calories as they use, weight remains stable. Regular exercise increases energy usage so it allows the person who exercises to consume more food without gaining weight. For example, an active 20-year-old woman needs to eat about 500 calories more per day to maintain weight than a sedentary woman of the same age, height, and weight. Choosing a diet rich in whole grains, fruits, and vegetables and moderate in fat maximizes nutrient intake without providing too many calories.

Body Mass Index (BMI)

Are you overweight or obese?

The Body Mass Index (BMI) is used to determine whether a person is at a healthy weight, overweight, or obese. BMI has some limitations, in that it can overestimate body fat in people who are very muscular and it can underestimate body fat in people who have lost muscle mass, such as many elderly.

Calculating your BMI $\text{Body Mass Index (BMI)} = \dfrac{\text{Weight (pounds)}}{\text{Height (inches)}^2} \times 703$

Body Mass Index (BMI) Chart

Weight (pounds)

Height	120	130	140	150	160	170	180	180	200	210	220	230	240	250
4'6"	29	31	34	36	39	41	43	46	48	51	53	56	58	60
4'8"	27	29	31	34	36	38	40	43	45	47	49	52	54	56
4'10"	25	27	29	31	34	36	38	40	42	44	46	48	50	52
5'0"	23	25	27	29	31	33	35	37	39	41	43	45	47	49
5'2"	22	24	26	27	29	31	33	35	37	38	40	42	44	46
5'4"	21	22	24	26	28	29	31	33	34	36	38	40	41	43
5'6"	19	21	23	24	26	27	29	31	32	34	36	37	39	40
5'8"	18	20	21	23	24	26	27	29	30	32	34	35	37	38
5'10"	17	19	20	22	23	24	26	27	29	30	32	33	35	36
6'	16	18	19	20	22	23	24	26	27	28	30	31	33	34
6'2"	15	17	18	19	21	22	23	24	26	27	28	30	31	32
6'4"	15	16	17	18	20	21	22	23	24	26	27	28	29	30
6'6"	14	15	16	17	19	20	21	22	23	24	25	27	28	29
6'8"	13	14	15	17	18	19	20	21	22	23	24	25	26	28

Underweight (<18.5) Overweight (25-29.9)

Healthy weight (18.5-24.9) Obese (30+)

Note: Chart is for Adults aged 20 and older.
Source: Office of the Surgeon General

FIGURE 1.2 The Body Mass Index is a popular way to indicate whether a person's weight is healthy for his or her height.

Heart Disease

Generally, when we use the term heart disease, we are talking about **atherosclerosis**. This is a condition in which fatty material builds up in the walls of the arteries. This causes the arteries to narrow and become less elastic. People with obesity, high blood pressure, high blood cholesterol levels, or diabetes are more likely to develop atherosclerosis. The risk of developing atherosclerosis also is increased by lifestyle choices, such as cigarette smoking, lack of exercise, and a diet high in saturated fat, cholesterol, and **trans** fat. Diets high in fiber, antioxidants (such as vitamins C and E), and fish and plant oils, which are high in healthy unsaturated fats, can reduce the risk of atherosclerosis. Adding exercise to this healthy mix further reduces risk.

Aerobic exercise decreases the risk of atherosclerosis by lowering blood pressure and increasing levels of a healthy type of blood cholesterol called HDL cholesterol. Aerobic exercise also strengthens the heart muscle, thereby lowering the resting heart rate and decreasing the heart's workload.

High Blood Pressure and Stroke

High blood pressure, or **hypertension**, can damage the blood vessels. This can increase the risk of atherosclerosis. If left untreated, high blood pressure may eventually lead to a stroke. A stroke occurs when there is a rupture or blockage of a blood vessel in the brain, shutting off blood flow to part of the brain. Blood pressure is increased by atherosclerosis, obesity, and diabetes. A healthy diet and exercise can lower blood pressure.

Diet affects blood pressure because many nutrients have a role in regulating blood pressure. Salt is perhaps the best known. Chemically, salt is sodium chloride. Although we use the terms salt and sodium interchangeably, it actually is the sodium that raises blood pressure. Diets high in salt are associated with a greater incidence of high blood pressure; reducing salt intake can help reduce blood pressure in many people. Low intakes of other nutrients—including calcium, magnesium, and potassium—have been associated with increases in blood pressure. A dietary pattern that is rich in the minerals calcium, magnesium, and potassium and moderate in sodium has been shown to help keep blood pressure in the healthy range. A diet that provides this pattern of nutrients is high in fruits and vegetables and includes whole grains, low-fat dairy products, and lean meats.

Maintaining a healthy weight is also important for healthy blood pressure. A weight loss of just 10 pounds (4.5 kilograms) can significantly lower blood pressure. Exercise helps promote and maintain weight loss. Increasing the amount of exercise, even without losing weight, can lower blood pressure by improving cardiovascular fitness and reducing stress.

CAN EXERCISE EXTEND LIFE?

Medical research has found that the more a body is used, the longer it lasts. A study of 17,000 Harvard alumni examined death rates over about 25 years. Men who exercised lived longer than those who didn't. Moderate exercise was found to reduce the risk of heart disease and to increase life expectancy slightly. But to achieve a real shot at longevity, work up a good sweat. Life expectancy was increased by two years in men who exercised strenuously at least two hours a week.

By "strenuous," the researchers meant a continuous workout of at least 20 to 30 minutes that increased heart rate to between 60% and 85% of its maximum. Strenuous activities include jogging, singles tennis, swimming, racquetball, biking, and aerobics classes. This amount of exercise was shown not only to lengthen life, but also to enhance cardiovascular fitness and reduce the risk of heart disease, hypertension, certain cancers, and diabetes.

Diabetes

Diabetes is a disease in which blood sugar levels are elevated. It occurs when there is not enough of the hormone insulin to remove glucose from the blood. Being overweight dramatically increases the risk of developing diabetes. Aerobic exercise can decrease the risk of developing diabetes by keeping body weight healthy. Exercise also makes the body respond better to insulin, reducing the amount that is needed to lower blood glucose. In people who already have diabetes, exercise can reduce or eliminate the need for medication, including insulin. Many scientists now believe that a dietary pattern that is high in refined carbohydrates and starches—such as sugar, white bread, pasta, and white rice—also may increase the long-term risk of developing diabetes. A diet that is low in refined starches and added sugars may reduce the risk of diabetes. This type of diet also helps maintain body weight in a healthy range.

Cancer

Cancer is caused by changes in a cell's genetic material. These changes can be caused by chemical reactions involving oxygen that damage cells, called oxidative damage. Both a healthy diet and exercise can reduce cancer risk. One of the reasons a proper diet protects against cancer is that certain vitamins and minerals, and chemicals found in plants called phytochemicals, are **antioxidants**. Antioxidants prevent oxidative damage to cells. A healthy diet also has other protective effects. For instance, vitamin A helps maintain a healthy immune system. A diet rich in calcium and vitamin D may protect against colon cancer. A diet high in fiber reduces the risks of colon, rectal, and breast cancers. Plenty of fluids may reduce the risk of bladder cancer. Certain phytochemicals also protect against cancer. They slow the growth of cancer cells and help cells to repair themselves. They also increase the activity of enzymes that prevent cancer and inhibit enzymes that promote cancer. A healthy diet also helps maintain a healthy weight, which reduces cancer risk. People who exercise regularly may further reduce their cancer risk. There is evidence that active people are less likely to develop colon and breast cancer than are their sedentary counterparts.

Osteoporosis and Arthritis

Did your parents tell you to drink your milk? That was good advice. Milk is a good source of calcium, as are peas and beans, fish eaten with bones (such as sardines), and leafy green vegetables. Adequate calcium throughout life helps develop dense, strong bones and keep them that way. Having dense bones reduces the likelihood of developing a bone disorder called **osteoporosis**. People with osteoporosis have fragile bones that can break easily. Exercise also prevents osteoporosis; the "use it or lose it" principle applies to bones as well as muscles. Regular weight-bearing exercise during childhood—such as walking, running, and jumping—can increase bone density. Weight-bearing exercise in adulthood can help prevent bone loss.

Arthritis occurs when the tissue that cushions the joints wears away over time. The bones of the joints rub together, causing pain. Exercise can help people with arthritis because increased strength and flexibility allows joints to move more easily.

HOW MUCH EXERCISE SHOULD YOU GET?

Despite all the health benefits of exercise, most Americans include very little activity in their daily lives. In fact, about one of every four American adults claims to get no physical activity during their leisure time. In order to maximize the benefits of exercise, it needs to be part of a daily routine. The most recent public health recommendations advise adults to get 150 minutes of moderately intense physical activity each week, or 75 minutes a week of vigorous activity. This amount will reduce the risk of many chronic diseases that are common among Americans today. Moderate exercise is equivalent in effort to walking briskly, and vigorous activity is equivalent in effort to running or jogging (Table 1.1). Greater health benefits can be obtained with up to 300 minutes of moderate-intensity exercise per week, or 150 minutes of vigorous activity. Sixty minutes of moderate to vigorous intensity exercise is recommended per day to maintain a healthy body weight. Sixty to 90 minutes per day may be needed to keep off weight that has been lost.

TABLE 1.1 EXAMPLES OF MODERATE AND VIGOROUS ACTIVITIES

Moderate-intensity activities	Walk briskly Play golf, pulling or carrying clubs Swim at a recreational pace Mow the lawn with a power mower Play doubles tennis Bicycle at 5 mph to 9 mph on level terrain or with a few hills Scrub floors or wash windows Lift weights (hydraulic machines or free weights)
Vigorous actives	Race-walk, jog, or run Swim laps Mow the lawn with a push mower Play singles tennis Bicycle at more than 10 mph, or on steep uphill terrain Move furniture Lift weights in circuit training

What Type of Exercise Is Best?

There is no one type of exercise that is best. As with diet, variety is key. Some activities should be aerobic, which improves cardiovascular and respiratory fitness. Some should be strength training, to enhance the strength and endurance of specific muscles. Choose enjoyable activities and mix them up. Bike one day, swim the next, and then spend a session lifting weights at the gym. Stretching also is important to promote and maintain flexibility. Time spent stretching does not count toward the goal of 150 minutes of physical activity per week.

To decrease the risk of injury, each exercise session should begin with a warm-up to increase blood flow to the muscles. Warm muscles are limber, and keeping muscles loose reduces the risk of injury and soreness. A five-minute warm-up of walking or rhythmic movement is recommended before starting any strenuous activity. A cool-down after the workout helps prevent muscle cramps and slowly brings down the heart rate.

WE'RE NOT MOVING

Any exercise is better than none, and within reason, more is better than less. Current physical activity guidelines recommend that adults get 150 minutes of activity per week and that children get 60 minutes per day. Unfortunately, more than 75% of Americans are not meeting this guideline. Many are not exercising at all. In a survey begun in 1988, about 31 of every 100 American adults reported that they were not active at all during their leisure time. When the survey was repeated in 2007, the U.S. Centers for Disease Control and Prevention reported improvement: Only 24 of every 100 adults reported being inactive. Unfortunately, if this many adults are sedentary, then 50 million people in the United States are at a significantly increased risk of developing chronic health problems due to inactivity.

Aerobic exercise, such as walking, bicycling, skating, swimming, or jogging, should be done for about 25 minutes to 60 minutes most days per week, depending on the intensity. For optimal benefit, aerobic activity should be performed at a level that keeps the heart rate between 60% and 85% of its maximum. Maximum heart rate is calculated by subtracting a person's age from 220. Therefore, a 20-year-old person would have a maximum heart rate of 200 beats per minute. He or she should exercise at a pace that keeps the heart rate between 120 and 170 beats per minute (Figure 1.3). A sedentary person beginning an exercise program may find that mild exercise, such as walking, can raise the heart rate into this range. As fitness improves, more intense activity is necessary to elevate heart rate to this level.

Resistance training, such as weight lifting, should be done two to three days a week at the start of an exercise program, and two days a week after the desired strength has been achieved. This can be done with weights or with resistance-exercise machines. Each session should include a minimum of 8 to 10 exercises that train the major muscle groups. Each exercise should be repeated 8 to 12 times. The weights should be heavy enough to cause the muscle to be near exhaustion after 8 to 12 repetitions. Increasing the amount of weight lifted will increase muscle strength. Increasing the number of repetitions will improve endurance.

To improve and maintain flexibility, stretching exercises should be done two to seven days a week. Muscles should be stretched to a position of mild discomfort and held for 10 to 30 seconds. Each stretch should be repeated three to five times.

How Much Should Children and Adolescents Exercise?

Children should be physically active for about 60 minutes per day. This activity should include aerobic exercise as well muscle-strengthening and bone-strengthening exercise. Children don't need to go to the gym. Muscle-strengthening activities include

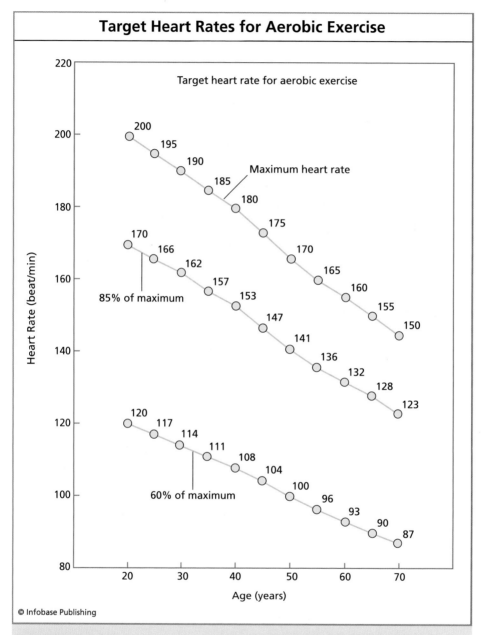

Target Heart Rates for Aerobic Exercise

© Infobase Publishing

FIGURE 1.3 Target heart rates differ by age and exercise goals. For low-intensity aerobic exercise, aim for 60% to 70% of maximum heart rate. Greater improvements in fitness and disease prevention can be achieved with higher intensity aerobic exercise, which is 70% to 80% of maximum heart rate.

climbing on playground equipment or playing tug-of-war. Bone-strengthening activities include jumping rope, playing hopscotch and basketball, and running. Activity for young children should include periods of moderate to vigorous activity lasting 10 to 15 minutes or more, followed by periods of rest. Children and adolescents can get their exercise by participating in fun activities with friends and family, such as playing tag, throwing a ball, or building a snow fort.

Most American children do not get the recommended amount of exercise. This is because television, computers, and video games often are chosen over physical activity. Studies have found that children who watch four or more hours of television per day have more body fat and a greater BMI than those who spend fewer than two hours watching television. Children who learn to enjoy physical activity are more likely to be active adults who maintain a healthy body weight and have a lower risk for disease. Learning by example is best. Children who have physically active parents are the leanest and the fittest.

REVIEW

A healthy lifestyle, which includes a nutritious diet and regular exercise, offers many health benefits. Following a healthy lifestyle makes it easier to maintain a proper body weight and keep muscles, bones, and joints strong. A nutritious diet provides the right number of calories to keep weight in a desirable range. It includes the proper balance of carbohydrates, protein, and fat; incorporates plenty of water; and provides enough (but not too much) vitamins and minerals. A healthy diet and adequate exercise can help prevent or delay conditions and diseases such as atherosclerosis, high blood pressure, stroke, diabetes, and cancer. It is recommended that adults engage in 150 minutes of moderate activity weekly and that children and teens exercise for an hour every day. A good exercise regimen should include aerobic exercise, strength training, and stretching exercises.

2

UNDERSTANDING AND MEETING NUTRIENT NEEDS

To eat a healthy diet, you need to understand the basics of **nutrition** and how this translates into food choices. The science of nutrition studies interactions between people and food. This includes how foods provide us with energy and the nutrients we need to stay alive, healthy, and active. An understanding of nutrition can help athletes select diets that provide the right amount of energy and nutrients to keep them healthy and optimize performance.

FOOD PROVIDES NUTRIENTS

People don't eat individual nutrients; they eat food. Food provides the body with energy and nutrients. It also contains other substances, such as chemicals found in plants called **phytochemicals**, which have not been defined as nutrients but have health-promoting properties. When a person chooses the right amounts and combinations of food, the resulting diet provides all of the nutrients and other substances needed to stay healthy. If a person chooses a poor combination of foods, he or she may miss out on some nutrients.

Choosing a diet that provides enough of all the nutrients we need can be challenging. People eat for many reasons besides obtaining nutrients. They eat because they see or smell a tempting food; because it's lunchtime; because they're at a party; because they are sad or happy; because it's Thanksgiving, and for a multitude of other reasons. Understanding what their needs are can help people choose a diet that meets these needs.

There are more than 40 nutrients necessary to human life. We need to consume these **essential nutrients** in our diets because the human body either cannot make them at all, or cannot make them in large enough amounts to optimize health. Different foods contain nutrients in varying amounts and combinations. For example, beef, chicken, and fish provide protein, vitamin B_6, and iron; bread, rice, and pasta provide carbohydrates, folic acid, and niacin; fruits and vegetables provide carbohydrates, fiber, vitamin A, and vitamin C; and vegetable oils provide fat and vitamin E. In addition to the nutrients found naturally in foods, some foods have nutrients added to them. **Fortification** adds nutrients to foods to replace losses that occur during cooking and processing, or to supplement the diet. Dietary supplements also are a source of nutrients. Although most people can meet their nutrient needs without supplements, they can be useful for maintaining health and preventing deficiencies.

WHAT NUTRIENTS DO

Nutrients provide three functions. Some nutrients provide energy. Some help form body structures. Some help to regulate the processes that keep us alive. Each nutrient performs one or more of these functions. All nutrients together are needed for growth, to maintain and repair the body, and to allow us to reproduce.

Energy

Nutrients provide the body with the energy, or fuel, that it needs to stay alive, to grow, and to move. This energy keeps the heart pumping, the lungs respiring, and the body warm. It also is used to keep the digestive tract churning and muscles working. Because carbohydrates, lipids, and proteins provide energy to the body, they are referred to as the **energy-yielding nutrients**. The energy used by the body is measured in **calories** or **kilocalories** (abbreviated as "kcalories" or "kcals"). In some other countries, food energy is measured in joules or **kilojoules** (abbreviated as "kjoules" or "kJs").

Each gram of carbohydrate provides the body with 4 calories. A gram of protein also provides 4 calories; a gram of fat provides 9 calories. For this reason, foods that are high in fat also are high in calories. Alcohol also provides energy, at 7 calories per gram, but alcohol is not considered a nutrient because the body does not need it to survive.

The more calories a person uses, the more he or she needs to eat in order to maintain weight (Figure 2.1). If people increase the

IS A CALORIE A KILOCALORIE?

There are 16 calories in a teaspoon of sugar. Yet, if in your chemistry class you measured the amount of energy in a teaspoon of sugar, the result would be about 16,000 calories, or 16 kilocalories. This is because the "calories" we use in nutrition to refer to the energy content of food are really kilocalories. A kilocalorie is 1,000 calories. Sometimes, as is the case on food labels, *calorie* is spelled with a capital "C" to indicate that it is referring to kilocalories. In the popular press, however, the term *calorie* with a lower case "c" is typically used to express the kilocalorie content of a food or of a diet. Therefore, when you eat a cookie that has 50 calories, keep in mind that it really has 50 kilocalories, or 50,000 calories.

FIGURE 2.1 People who frequently exercise burn more calories and can eat more without gaining weight than people who lead a more inactive lifestyle.

amount they exercise without increasing the amount they eat, they will lose weight. People who eat more without exercising more will gain weight because their bodies will store the extra energy, mostly as body fat. People who consume the same number of calories as they use are in **energy balance**, and body weight remains stable.

Structure

There is truth to the saying, "You are what you eat." The structures in the human body are formed from nutrients consumed in the diet. By weight, a person's body is about 60% water, 16% protein, 16% fat, and 6% minerals. The minerals calcium and phosphorus make bones and teeth hard. Protein forms the structure of tendons, ligaments, and muscles. Lipids are the major structural component of the membranes that surround body cells. Water is a structural nutrient because it plumps up cells, giving them shape.

Regulation

All of the processes that occur in the body—from the breakdown of carbohydrates and fat to provide energy to the building of bone and muscle to form body structures—must be regulated in order to allow the body to function normally. Conditions in the body must be kept within certain limits to support life. For instance, the processes that maintain body temperature around 98.6°F (37°C) are regulated so body temperature does not rise above or fall below the healthy range. The constant internal body environment is called **homeostasis**. Maintaining homeostasis requires many nutrients. Water helps to regulate body temperature. Lipids and proteins are needed to make regulatory molecules called hormones. Proteins, vitamins, and minerals help regulate the rate of chemical reactions within the body.

GETTING NUTRIENTS TO CELLS

To obtain nutrients the body needs to break down food and then transport the nutrients it provides to cells. Digestion breaks down

Digestive System

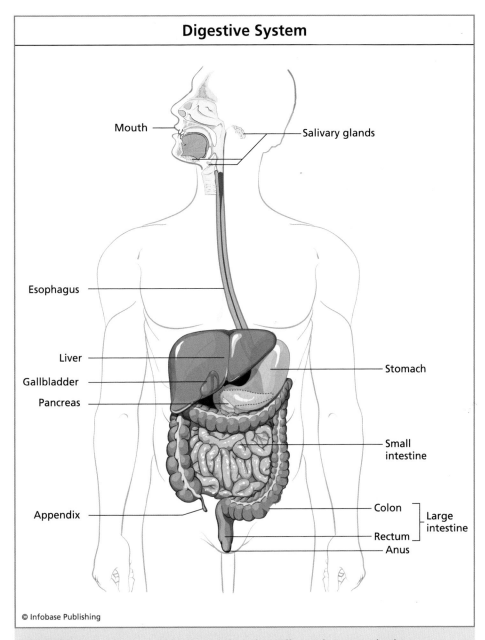

Mouth

Salivary glands

Esophagus

Liver

Gallbladder

Pancreas

Stomach

Small intestine

Appendix

Colon

Large intestine

Rectum

Anus

© Infobase Publishing

FIGURE 2.2 After food is chewed and swallowed, it travels down the esophagus to the stomach, where it is further broken down and prepared for entry into the small intestine. In the small intestine, most digestion occurs and nutrients are absorbed into the bloodstream.

food. Absorption brings the nutrients into the blood, so they can be transported to the cells where they are needed.

The digestive system is responsible for both digestion and absorption (Figure 2.2). The main part of this system is the **gastrointestinal tract**, also called the GI tract. This hollow tube starts at the mouth, where chewing breaks food into small pieces. From there, food passes down the esophagus into the

BACTERIA IN YOUR INTESTINE

Did you know that your large intestine is home to several hundred species of bacteria? You provide them with a nice, warm home with lots of food. They do some favors in return. These bacteria improve the digestion and absorption of nutrients. They make some vitamins. They break down harmful substances, such as ammonia. They help your immune system work, and are responsible for the proper growth of cells in the large intestine. A healthy population of intestinal bacteria may also help prevent constipation, gas, and excess stomach acid. However, if the wrong bacteria take over, the result could be diarrhea, infections, and perhaps an increased risk of cancer.

How can you make sure the right bacteria are in your gut? One way is to eat them. This is referred to as **probiotic** therapy. Live bacteria are found in foods such as yogurt and acidophilus milk and can be purchased as bottled suspensions or tablets. One problem with probiotic therapy is that the bacteria are washed out of the large intestine if the person stops eating them. A second approach that can modify the bacteria in the gut is to consume foods or other substances that encourage the growth of particular types of bacteria. Substances that pass into the large intestine and serve as food for these bacteria are called **prebiotics**. Prebiotics are sold as dietary supplements, but don't run to the store just yet. For most people eating a healthy diet will ensure a healthy population of intestinal bacteria.

stomach, and then on to the small intestine. Rhythmic contractions of the smooth muscles that line the GI tract help mix food and move it along. Digestive **enzymes** in the gastrointestinal tract break down the nutrients in food. The digestive system also secretes hormones into the blood that help regulate GI activity. Most of the digestion and absorption of nutrients occurs in the small intestine. Anything that is not absorbed passes into the large intestine. Here, water and small amounts of some other nutrients can be absorbed, and waste is prepared for elimination.

HOW YOUR BODY USES NUTRIENTS

Once inside body cells, carbohydrates, lipids, and proteins are involved in chemical reactions that break them down to provide energy or use them to build other substances that the human body needs. The sum of these chemical reactions that occur inside body cells is called **metabolism**. The chemical reactions of metabolism can synthesize the molecules needed to form body structures such as muscles, nerves, and bones. The reactions of metabolism also break down carbohydrates, lipids, and proteins to yield energy in the form of **ATP (adenosine triphosphate)**. ATP is a high-energy molecule that is used by cells as an energy source to do work, such as to pump blood, contract muscles, or synthesize new body tissue.

THE SIX CLASSES OF NUTRIENTS

The nutrients we need come from six different classes: carbohydrates, lipids, protein, water, vitamins, and minerals (Table 2.1). Each class, with the exception of water, contains a variety of different molecules that the body uses in different ways. Some classes of nutrients are needed in relatively large amounts, whereas others meet needs when only tiny amounts are consumed. Carbohydrates, lipids, protein, and water are often referred to as macronutrients because they are required in the diet in relatively large amounts. Vitamins and minerals are referred to as micronutrients because they are needed in only small amounts in the diet.

TABLE 2.1 CATEGORIES OF NUTRIENTS

Nutrient Category	Nutrients Included
Macronutrients	
Carbohydrates	Sugars, starches, and fiber
Protein	Proteins and amino acids
Lipids	Triglycerides, Fatty Acids, phosphoglycerides (phospholipids), and sterols (including cholesterol)
Water	Water
Micronutrients	
Vitamins	*Fat soluble vitamins:* Vitamins A, D, E, and K *Water soluble vitamins:* Vitamins C, B_6, B_{12}, Thiamin, Riboflavin, Folate, Niacin, Pantothenic acid, and Biotin
Minerals	*Major minerals:* Sodium, Potassium, Chloride, Calcium, Phosphorus, Magnesium, and Sulfur *Trace minerals:* Iron, Copper, Zinc, Manganese, Selenium, Iodine, Fluoride, Chromium, and Molybdenum

Carbohydrates

Carbohydrates include sugars, **starches**, and **fiber**. Sugars are the simplest form of carbohydrate. They are made up of one or two sugar units. They taste sweet and are found in fruit, milk, and sweeteners like honey and table sugar. Starches are made of many sugar units linked together. They do not taste sweet, and are found in cereals, grains, and starchy vegetables like potatoes. Starches and sugars are good sources of energy in the diet and provide 4 calories per gram. Most fiber is also carbohydrate. Good sources of fiber include whole grains, legumes (peas and beans), fruits, and vegetables. Fiber provides little energy to the body because it cannot be digested or absorbed. It is, however, important for the health of the gastrointestinal tract.

Lipids

Lipids are commonly called fat. Fat is a concentrated source of energy in our diet and in our bodies, providing 9 calories per gram of fat. Most of the fat in our diet and in our body is in the form of **triglycerides**. Each triglyceride contains three **fatty acids**. Fatty acids are basically long, short, or medium length chains of carbon atoms. Depending on how these carbons are linked together, fats are classified as either **saturated fats** or **unsaturated fats**. Saturated fats are usually solid at room temperature and are found mostly in animal products such as meat, milk, and butter. Unsaturated fats are found in vegetable oils and are usually liquid at room temperature. Small amounts of certain unsaturated fatty acids are essential in the diet. **Cholesterol** is another type of lipid. It is found in animal foods, but not in plants. Diets high in saturated fat and cholesterol may increase the risk of heart disease. A type of unsaturated fat called trans fat should also be limited because it promotes heart disease.

Protein

Protein is needed for growth, for the maintenance and repair of body structures, and for the synthesis of regulatory molecules. It can also be broken down to provide energy (4 calories per gram of protein). Proteins are made of folded chains of units called **amino acids**. The number and order of amino acids in the chain determine the type of protein. The right amounts and types of amino acids must be consumed in the diet in order to meet the body's protein needs. Animal foods such as meat, poultry, fish, eggs, and dairy products generally supply a combination of amino acids that meets human needs better than plant proteins. However, vegetarian diets that contain only plant foods such as grains, nuts, seeds, vegetables, and legumes, can also meet protein needs.

Water

Water is an essential nutrient that makes up about 60% of the weight of an adult human body. It provides no energy but is needed in the body to transport nutrients, oxygen, waste products, and other important substances. It also is needed for many chemical reactions, for body structure, lubrication, and protection, and to regulate body temperature. Water is found in beverages as well as solid foods. Water is not stored in the body, so to maintain proper hydration water intake must balance water losses in urine, feces, sweat, and from evaporation.

Vitamins

Vitamins are small carbon-based molecules needed to regulate metabolic processes. They are found in almost all the foods we eat but no one food is a good source of all of them. Some vitamins are soluble in water and others are soluble in fat (see Table 2.1), a property that affects how they are absorbed into and transported throughout the body. Vitamins do not provide energy but many are needed to regulate the chemical reactions that extract energy from sugars, fatty acids, and amino acids. Some vitamins are antioxidants, which protect the body from reactive oxygen compounds like free radicals. Others have roles in tissue growth and development, bone health, and blood clot formation.

Minerals

Minerals are single elements such as iron, calcium, zinc, and copper (See Table 2.1). Some are needed in the diet in significant amounts, whereas the requirements for others are extremely small. Like vitamins, minerals provide no energy but perform a number of very diverse functions. Some are needed to regulate chemical reactions, some participate in reactions that protect cells from oxidative damage, and others have roles in bone formation and maintenance, oxygen transport, or immune function.

HOW MUCH OF EACH NUTRIENT DO YOU NEED?

To stay healthy, adequate amounts of energy and of each of the essential nutrients must be consumed in the diet. The exact amount of each that you need depends on your age, size, sex, genetic makeup, lifestyle, and health status. The **Dietary Reference Intakes (DRIs)** are general recommendations for the amounts of energy (calories), nutrients, and other substances that should be consumed on an average daily basis in order to promote health, prevent deficiencies, and reduce the incidence of chronic disease.

The Dietary Reference Intakes (DRIs)

The DRIs include recommendations for different groups of people based on age, gender, and, when appropriate, pregnancy and lactation. The recommendations for nutrient intakes include four different types of values. The **Estimated Average Requirements (EARs)** are the amounts of nutrients that are estimated to meet the average needs of the population. They are not used to assess individual intake but rather are intended for planning and evaluating the adequacy of the nutrient intake of population groups. The **Recommended Dietary Allowances (RDAs)** and **Adequate**

Intakes (AIs) are values that are calculated to meet the needs of nearly all healthy people in each gender and life-stage group. These can be used to plan and assess individual's diets. The fourth set of DRI values is the **Tolerable Upper Intake Levels (ULs)**. These are the maximum levels of intake that are unlikely to pose a risk of adverse health effects. ULs can be used as a guide to limit intake and evaluate the possibility of excessive intake. When your diet provides the RDA or AI for each nutrient and does not exceed the UL for any, your risk of nutrient deficiency or toxicity is low.

The recommendations for energy intake are expressed as **Estimated Energy Requirements (EERs)**. These values predict the calories needed to maintain weight in healthy individuals. They are based on age, gender, body size, and activity level. Formulas for calculating EERs are included in Chapter 5 and Appendix A.

What Happens If You Get Too Little or Too Much?

Consuming either too much or too little of one or more nutrients or energy can cause **malnutrition**. Typically, we think of malnutrition as a lack of energy or nutrients. This may occur if someone doesn't include enough in their diet, but it is also caused by an increase in energy or nutrient requirements, or an inability to absorb or use nutrients.

Energy deficiency is called starvation. It causes a loss of body fat and muscle mass, resulting in an emaciated appearance. Malnutrition due to individual nutrient deficiencies causes symptoms that reflect the functions of the nutrient in the body. For example, vitamin D is needed for strong bones. A deficiency of this vitamin causes the leg bones of children to bow outward because they are too weak to support their body weight. Vitamin A is needed for healthy eyes; a deficiency can result in blindness. For many nutrient deficiencies, supplying the lacking nutrient can quickly reverse the symptoms.

Overnutrition, an excess of energy or nutrients, is also a form of malnutrition. An excess of energy causes obesity. It increases the risk of developing diseases such as diabetes and heart disease.

Excesses of vitamins and minerals rarely occur from eating food but are seen with overuse of dietary supplements. For example, consuming too much vitamin B_6 can cause nerve damage and excess iron intake can cause liver failure.

TOOLS FOR CHOOSING A HEALTHY DIET

Knowing which nutrients your body needs to stay healthy is the first step in choosing a healthy diet, but knowing how many milligrams of niacin, micrograms of vitamin B_{12}, grams of fiber, or what percent of calories from carbohydrates should be included in a healthy diet doesn't help you decide what to eat for breakfast or pack for lunch. A variety of tools has been developed to help you make these kinds of choices. Discussions of three of them—standardized food labels, the Dietary Guidelines for Americans, and MyPyramid—follow.

Understanding Food Labels

Food labels are a tool designed to help consumers make healthy food choices. They provide information about the nutrient

TOO MUCH OF A GOOD THING CAN KILL YOU

We usually think of the vitamins and minerals in our supplements as a healthy addition to our diets, but too much can be dangerous. Consuming too much of a nutrient from dietary supplements can cause problems, including nerve damage, kidney stones, liver and heart damage, and, in extreme cases, death. For example, high doses of vitamin B_6 can cause tingling, numbness, and muscle weakness; high doses of niacin causes flushing; and too much vitamin C can cause diarrhea. Overdosing on iron from children's vitamin/mineral supplements is one of the leading causes of poisoning in children under the age of six. To be safe, take supplements according to the recommended doses and use the ULs from the DRIs to check for toxic doses.

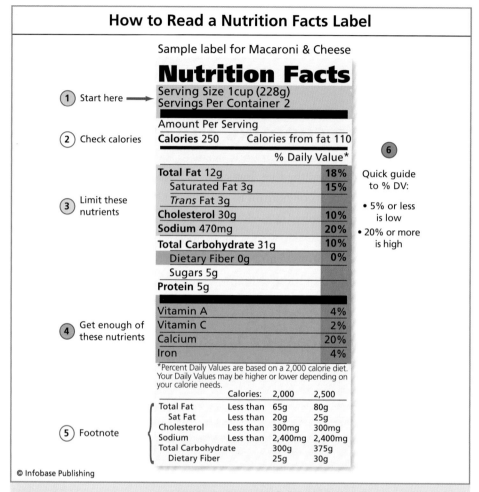

How to Read a Nutrition Facts Label

Sample label for Macaroni & Cheese

Nutrition Facts

Serving Size 1cup (228g)
Servings Per Container 2

Amount Per Serving

Calories 250   Calories from fat 110

% Daily Value*

Total Fat 12g	**18%**
Saturated Fat 3g	**15%**
Trans Fat 3g	
Cholesterol 30g	**10%**
Sodium 470mg	**20%**
Total Carbohydrate 31g	**10%**
Dietary Fiber 0g	**0%**
Sugars 5g	
Protein 5g	

Vitamin A	4%
Vitamin C	2%
Calcium	20%
Iron	4%

*Percent Daily Values are based on a 2,000 calorie diet.
Your Daily Values may be higher or lower depending on
your calorie needs.

		Calories:	2,000	2,500
Total Fat	Less than		65g	80g
Sat Fat	Less than		20g	25g
Cholesterol	Less than		300mg	300mg
Sodium	Less than		2,400mg	2,400mg
Total Carbohydrate			300g	375g
Dietary Fiber			25g	30g

(1) Start here

(2) Check calories

(3) Limit these nutrients

(4) Get enough of these nutrients

(5) Footnote

(6) Quick guide to % DV:

• 5% or less is low

• 20% or more is high

© Infobase Publishing

FIGURE 2.3 A "Nutrition Facts" label lists the calories and amounts of nutrients in a single food serving. These labels appear on all packaged foods and can help consumers plan their diet.

composition of individual foods and show how a serving of the food fits into the recommendations for a healthy diet.

Almost all packaged foods must carry a standard food label. Exceptions are raw fruits, vegetables, fish, meat, and poultry. For these foods, the nutrition information is often posted on placards in the grocery store or printed in brochures. Food labels must include both an ingredient list and a "Nutrition Facts" panel.

The ingredient list is a listing all of the substances contained in the food, including food additives, colors, and flavorings. The ingredients are listed in order of their prominence by weight. Therefore a label that lists water first indicates that most of the weight of that food comes from water. You can look at the ingredient list if you are trying to avoid certain ingredients, such as animal products, or a food to which you have an allergy.

The "Nutrition Facts" portion of a food label (Figure 2.3) lists the serving size of the food followed by the total calories, calories from fat, and amounts of total fat, saturated fat, trans fat, cholesterol, sodium, total carbohydrates, dietary fiber, sugars, and protein per serving of the food. The amounts of all of these nutrients are given by weight and for most, also as a percent of the Daily Value. Daily Values (DV) are standards developed for food labels. They are based on a 2,000-calorie diet. They help consumers see how a food fits into their overall diet. For example, if a food provides 10% of the Daily Value for fiber, then the food provides 10% of the daily recommendation for fiber intake in a 2,000-calorie diet. The amounts of vitamin A, vitamin C, iron, and calcium are also listed as a percent of the Daily Value.

In addition to the required nutrition information, food labels often highlight specific characteristics of a product that might be of interest to the consumer, such as advertising that a food is "low in fat" or "high in fiber." The Food and Drug Administration (FDA) has developed definitions for these nutrient content descriptors. For example, to be "low in calories" a food must contain no more than 40 calories per serving. Food labels are also permitted to include specific health claims if they are relevant to the product. For example, the label on oatmeal may claim that it helps to lower blood cholesterol. Health claims are only permitted on labels if the scientific evidence for the claim is reviewed by the FDA and found to be strong.

The Dietary Guidelines

The Dietary Guidelines for Americans include recommendations designed to help you choose a diet and lifestyle that will

---

TABLE 2.2 KEY RECOMMENDATIONS OF THE DIETARY GUIDELINES FOR AMERICANS, 2005

- Consume a variety of foods within and among the various food groups.
- Balance calorie intake with expenditure to manage body weight.
- Be physically active every day.
- Choose more fruits and vegetables, whole grains, and low-fat dairy products.
- Choose fats wisely.
- Choose fiber-rich carbohydrates and limit added sugars.
- Choose and prepare foods with little salt.
- If you drink alcoholic beverages, do so in moderation.
- Prepare, handle, and store food safely.

---

promote health and reduce chronic disease risks. The Dietary Guidelines recommend choosing a variety of nutrient-dense foods. These include vegetables, fruits, whole grains, low-fat dairy products, lean meats, beans, nuts, and seeds. This type of diet is rich in fiber, micronutrients, and phytochemicals, and low in saturated fat. The key recommendations of the Dietary Guidelines (see Table 2.2) are appropriate for all healthy Americans two years of age and older.

MyPyramid

MyPyramid is a tool designed to help consumers choose foods that meet the recommendations of the Dietary Guidelines. This food guide divides foods into five food groups (grains, vegetables, fruits, milk, and meat and beans) and oils based on the nutrients they provide. The five food groups and oils are represented by the colored triangles that make up the pyramid. The shape of the colored pyramids helps emphasize the recommendations for the amounts and types of food from each of the five food groups (Figure 2.4); the wider the pyramid, the greater the proportion of food from that group. Foods in the wider base of each triangle contain the most nutrients per calorie; those in the narrow tip are lower in nutrients per calorie. The figure climbing the pyramid steps emphasizes the importance of activity in maintaining nutritional health. Choosing the recommended amounts and varieties of foods from each group will provide a

FOOD GROUPS BY THE NUMBERS

Using a food group system to like MyPyramid to guide food intake in the United States is not new. The first food group system, or food guide, was published in 1916. It was called Food for Young Children and divided food into five groups: milk/meat, cereals, vegetables/fruits, fats/fatty foods, and sugars/sugary foods. During the Great Depression, a food guide consisting of 12 food groups was developed and released to help families save money on groceries. In 1943, shortages brought on by World War II led to the release of a food guide called the "Basic Seven." Because of the complexity of the Basic Seven, in 1956 it was condensed to the Basic Four. The Basic Four included milk, meats, fruits and vegetables, and grain products and was used for the next 20 years. In the late 1970s, as concerns about chronic disease began to intensify, the USDA added a fifth category to the Basic Four: fats, sweets, and alcoholic beverages, that people were advised to consume in moderation. In 1992, the Food Guide Pyramid was introduced. It used a pyramid shape to emphasize the relative contribution that 6 food groups should make to a healthy diet. It was replaced by MyPyramid in 2005.

Food guides are not unique to the United States. Those developed in other countries use a variety of shapes and numbers of groups to emphasize the proportions of different types of foods that should make up a healthy diet. Korea and China use a pagoda shape, Mexico, Australia, and most European countries use a pie or plate shape, and Canada uses a rainbow.

MyPyramid
STEPS TO A HEALTHIER YOU
MyPyramid.gov

| GRAINS | VEGETABLES | FRUITS | MILK | MEAT & BEANS |

GRAINS	VEGETABLES	FRUITS	MILK	MEAT & BEANS
Make half your grains whole	Vary your veggies	Focus on fruits	Get your calcium-rich foods	Go lean with protein
Eat at least 3 oz. of whole-grain cereals, breads, crackers, rice, or pasta every day 1 oz. is about 1 slice of bread, about 1 cup of breakfast cereal, or 1/2 cup of cooked rice, cereal, or pasta	Eat more dark-green veggies like broccoli, spinach, and other dark leafy greens Eat more orange vegetables like carrots and sweetpotatoes Eat more dry beans and peas like pinto beans, kidney beans, and lentils	Eat a variety of fruit Choose fresh, frozen, canned, or dried fruit Go easy on fruit juices	Go low-fat or fat-free when you choose milk, yogurt, and other milk products If you don't or can't consume milk, choose lactose-free products or other calcium sources such as fortified foods and beverages	Choose low-fat or lean meats and poultry Bake it, broil it, or grill it Vary your protein routine — choose more fish, beans, peas, nuts, and seeds

For a 2,000-calorie diet, you need the amounts below from each food group. To find the amounts that are right for you, go to MyPyramid.gov.

| Eat 6 oz. every day | Eat 2 1/2 cups every day | Eat 2 cups every day | Get 3 cups every day; for kids aged 2 to 8, it's 2 | Eat 5 1/2 oz. every day |

Find your balance between food and physical activity
- Be sure to stay within your daily calorie needs.
- Be physically active for at least 30 minutes most days of the week.
- About 60 minutes a day of physical activity may be needed to prevent weight gain.
- For sustaining weight loss, at least 60 to 90 minutes a day of physical activity may be required.
- Children and teenagers should be physically active for 60 minutes every day, or most days.

Know the limits on fats, sugars, and salt (sodium)
- Make most of your fat sources from fish, nuts, and vegetable oils.
- Limit solid fats like butter, margarine, shortening, and lard, as well as foods that contain these.
- Check the Nutrition Facts label to keep saturated fats, trans fats, and sodium low.
- Choose food and beverages low in added sugars. Added sugars contribute calories with few, if any, nutrients.

MyPyramid.gov
STEPS TO A HEALTHIER YOU

U.S. Department of Agriculture
Center for Nutrition Policy and Promotion
April 2005
CNPP-15

USDA

diet that meets the recommendations for an adequate diet that will help promote health, prevent disease, and support physical activity.

Find your MyPyramid plan by going to www.mypyramid. gov, selecting "MyPyramid Plan," and entering your age, gender, and activity level. The MyPyramid Web site also provides other interactive tools to help users identify their calorie needs, choose nutrient-dense foods, plan healthy diets, analyze meals, and estimate the calories they expend in activity.

REVIEW

Food provides our bodies with energy, in the form of calories, and nutrients, which are substances required in the diet for growth, reproduction, and maintenance of our bodies. The right number of calories is needed to keep weight in the healthy range and the right combination of nutrients is needed to maintain health. There are six classes of nutrients. Carbohydrates include sugars, starches, and fibers. Sugars and starches provide energy, 4 calories per gram. Fibers provide little energy because they cannot be digested by human enzymes and therefore cannot be absorbed. Lipids are a concentrated source of calories in the diet and in the body, providing 9 calories per gram. They are also needed to synthesize molecules that provide structure and help regulate body processes. Proteins are made from amino acids. In the body, proteins can provide energy but their structural and regulatory roles are more important. Water is the most abundant nutrient in the body. Water intake must equal output to maintain balance. Vitamins and minerals are needed in the diet in small amounts. They both have regulatory roles and some

FIGURE 2.4 *(opposite)* MyPyramid provides recommendations designed to help people maintain a healthy lifestyle.

minerals also provide structure. Consuming too much or too little energy or nutrients results in malnutrition. The Dietary Reference Intakes (DRIs) recommend amounts of energy and nutrients needed to promote health, prevent deficiencies, and reduce the incidence of chronic disease. Food labels, the Dietary Guidelines for Americans, and MyPyramid provide information and recommendations that help people choose foods that make up a healthy diet.

3

UNDERSTANDING WHAT HAPPENS WHEN WE EXERCISE

When people exercise they use more energy. To provide this energy to muscle cells, some systems are stimulated to help the muscles do their work, while others are turned down to conserve energy. The heart and lungs work harder to help supply oxygen to the muscles and eliminate waste products. At the same time, the digestive system slows so that it does not burn energy that could be used to fuel the muscles. These are normal responses to exercise, whether the person exercising is a competitive athlete or just out for some weekend fun. The systems most affected are the muscles and the systems involved in delivering oxygen to the muscles.

ENERGY FOR EXERCISE

The molecule that provides energy for the contraction of exercising muscles is called ATP (adenosine triphosphate). ATP is the immediate source of energy for all body functions. It supplies the energy needed to breathe, circulate blood, eliminate body wastes, and maintain body temperature. It also supplies the energy for muscle contraction, whether the muscles are needed to do homework, walk to class, or compete in a track meet. ATP for muscle contraction is produced inside the muscle cells, primarily from the breakdown of glucose and fatty acids. During vigorous exercise, ATP is produced and consumed rapidly by the muscles. If exercise is more leisurely, ATP is produced and consumed more slowly.

ATP can be produced in different ways. One way is called **aerobic metabolism**. This type of metabolism requires oxygen. Aerobic exercise, such as jogging, biking, or swimming, relies on aerobic metabolism and therefore requires oxygen. Aerobic metabolism produces ATP slowly, but it is very efficient: It produces a great deal of ATP from each molecule of glucose. Aerobic metabolism also can produce ATP from fatty acids. People store so much energy as body fat that there is always fat available as an energy source.

ATP can also be produced in the absence of oxygen at the cell, which occurs (among other times) during high-intensity exercise, such as sprinting. This **anaerobic metabolism** produces ATP very quickly. But anaerobic metabolism produces fewer ATP molecules from each glucose molecule than aerobic metabolism does, and it cannot use fatty acids. Therefore, relying on anaerobic metabolism uses up fuel, that is glucose, very rapidly. When glucose stores are depleted, it is not possible to continue exercising at the same intensity level, and the person feels **fatigue**. People with a greater ability to deliver oxygen to the muscles (and for the muscles to use this oxygen to generate ATP by aerobic metabolism) can perform more intense exercise before feeling fatigue. A person's ability to deliver oxygen to muscles and use aerobic metabolism to generate energy is referred to as his or her **aerobic capacity.** It also is referred to as **maximal oxygen consumption**, or **VO$_2$max**. Someone with a greater aerobic capacity can exercise at a higher intensity for a longer time.

GETTING OXYGEN TO MUSCLE CELLS

The respiratory system consists of the lungs and air passageways. The cardiovascular system includes the heart and blood vessels.

Organ Systems

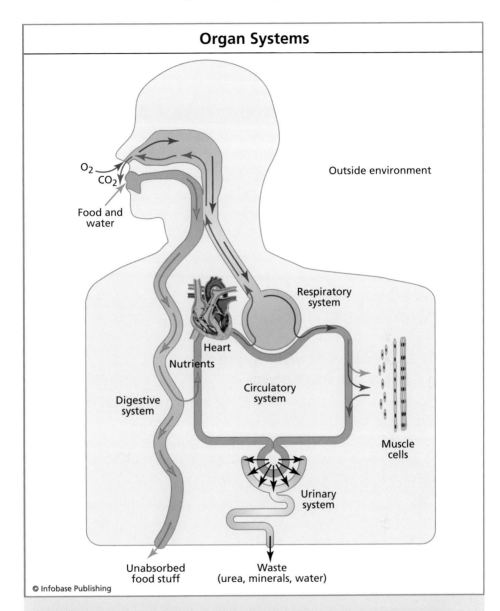

FIGURE 3.1 The organ systems of the body are closely related. The digestive system takes in nutrients while the respiratory system takes in oxygen. Nutrients and oxygen are then distributed to the muscles and other body cells by the circulatory system. At the same time, the circulatory system also carries waste from the cells to the lungs and urinary system to be eliminated from the body.

Together, these two systems bring oxygen into the body and deliver it to tissues, including the exercising muscles. They also help eliminate waste products from the same tissues (Figure 3.1).

The Respiratory System: Take a Breath

When you inhale, the respiratory system brings oxygen into your body. Air enters through the nose or mouth and travels down the trachea to branching passageways in the lungs. There, oxygen from the air is transferred to the bloodstream and carbon dioxide is transferred from the blood to the air. Most of the oxygen in the blood is bound to the protein hemoglobin, which is found in red blood cells. Hemoglobin acts like a delivery truck, transporting oxygen from the lungs to tissues throughout the body. Hemoglobin also transports carbon dioxide from the tissues to the lungs so it can be eliminated in exhaled air.

The Cardiovascular System: It Keeps on Pumping

The cardiovascular system includes your heart and blood vessels. It circulates blood, which transports oxygen and nutrients to all the body cells. The heart pumps blood through the body. It is a muscular pump with two circulatory loops. One delivers blood to the lungs, and one delivers blood to the rest of the body.

The blood vessels that carry blood toward the heart are called veins, and those that carry blood away from the heart are called arteries. As arteries carry blood away from the heart, they branch many times, forming smaller and smaller blood vessels. The smallest arteries then branch to form **capillaries**, which are thin-walled vessels that are just large enough to allow one red blood cell to pass through at a time. The thin walls of the capillaries allow the exchange of nutrients and gases. In the capillaries of the lungs, blood brings carbon dioxide to be exhaled and picks up oxygen to be delivered to the cells. In the capillaries of the GI tract, blood delivers oxygen and picks up water-soluble nutrients absorbed from the diet. From the capillaries, blood flows into the smallest veins, which converge to form larger and larger veins for return to the heart. To summarize, oxygen-poor blood is pumped through arteries to the capillaries of the lungs, where it picks up oxygen. It then returns to the heart via veins, and is pumped out again through the arteries that lead to the rest of the body. In the capillaries of the body, blood delivers oxygen and nutrients and removes wastes. It then returns to the heart via veins.

HOW IS OXYGEN DELIVERY INCREASED?

During exercise, the body uses more oxygen than it does at rest. A number of adaptations occur during exercise to increase blood flow and the amount of oxygen delivered to the muscles.

Deeper, More Frequent Breaths

The need for more oxygen causes an increase in the depth and rate of breathing. At rest, about 250 milliliters of oxygen is transferred from the lungs to the blood each minute, and about 200 milliliters of carbon dioxide moves from the blood to the lungs

HOW MUCH BLOOD CAN A HEART PUMP?

During maximum exercise, heart rate in both trained and untrained people is about the same. In young men, for example, it is about 195 beats per minute. However, trained athletes pump a great deal more blood with each heart beat, because training has increased stroke volume. During exercise, stroke volume is almost three quarters of a cup (179 mL) in trained men, compared with less than a half a cup (113 mL) in untrained men. A trained man's heart can pump about 9.2 gallons (almost 35 L) of blood per minute, compared with only about 5.8 gallons (22 L) in an untrained man. The increased blood flow increases the amount of oxygen that can be delivered to cells during exercise, allowing the cells to produce ATP more efficiently.

to be exhaled. During exercise, this exchange can increase up to 25 times more. The increased breathing rate helps ensure that more oxygen can be picked up and more carbon dioxide expelled.

A Faster Heart

The total amount of blood pumped increases with exercise. The amount of blood pumped by the heart during a one-minute period is called **cardiac output**. Cardiac output depends on heart rate, which is how fast the heart beats, and **stroke volume**, which is how much blood the heart pumps with each beat. At rest, the heart of an average male college student beats about 70 times per minute, and stroke volume is about a third of a cup (71 mL). This results in a cardiac output of about 23 cups (5,000 mL) per minute. During high-intensity exercise, heart rate would increase to about 195 beats per minute and stroke volume to almost a half a cup (113 mL), resulting in a cardiac output of 98 cups (22,000 mL), or about 6 gallons (22 L) per minute!

Changing Blood Flow

Exercise also affects how oxygen-rich blood is distributed. The volume of blood that flows to an organ or tissue depends on need. Blood vessels can either constrict or dilate to allow blood to be rapidly redistributed. As a person exercises, the blood vessels in active muscles dilate to increase the blood supply, while the blood vessels that supply the kidneys, liver, pancreas, and gastrointestinal tract constrict. At rest, about 24% of blood flow goes to the digestive system, 20% to skeletal muscles, and the rest to the heart, kidneys, brain, skin, and other organs. During strenuous exercise, more than 70% of blood flow will be directed to the skeletal muscles (Figure 3.2).

A Change in the Muscle

During exercise, metabolic reactions in working muscles generate acids. The increase in acidity reduces the attraction between oxygen and hemoglobin. This reduced attraction allows the hemo-

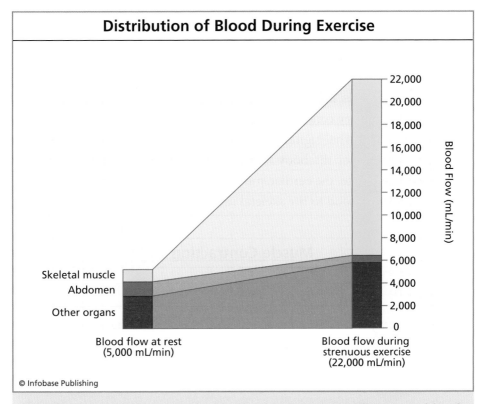

FIGURE 3.2 When exercising, the circulatory system will increase blood flow and adjust the amount of blood delivered to certain areas of the body. Because the exercising muscles are more in need of oxygen, more blood will be distributed to them, while less will travel towards the abdomen and other organs.

globin in the blood to release more oxygen, which increases the amount of oxygen picked up by the muscle cells.

HOW DO MUSCLES WORK?

The human body has three types of muscles. The type used to walk up a flight of stairs, run around a track, or swim laps in a pool is called **skeletal muscle**. Skeletal muscles are attached to the bones of the skeleton and are under voluntary control: They move when the person wants them to move. These muscles are responsible for all voluntary movement. There are more than 600 skeletal muscles in the body. During exercise, the activity of the skeletal muscles increases.

The heart is made of **cardiac muscle**. Cardiac muscle is not under voluntary control. The heart beats, whether people want it to or not. Internal signals adjust the heart rate to meet the oxygen demands of the body tissues and to maintain homeostasis. During exercise, the cardiac muscles work harder to deliver more oxygen-rich blood to the skeletal muscles.

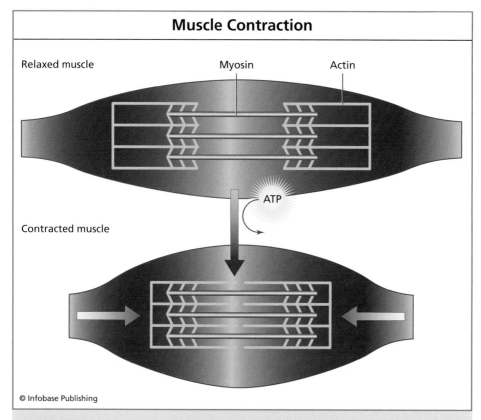

Muscle Contraction

Relaxed muscle   Myosin   Actin

Contracted muscle

ATP

© Infobase Publishing

FIGURE 3.3 All three types of muscles—cardiac, skeletal, and smooth—contract through the use of myofibrils, which are made up of two types of filaments called myosin and actin.

The third type of muscle is called **smooth muscle**. It lines the vessels that deliver blood to body cells, the air passageways in and out of the lungs, and the walls of digestive tract, glands, and other organs. This type of muscle also is involuntary muscle; its contractions and relaxations are not under conscious control. Smooth muscle plays an important role during exercise. For example, it is the smooth muscles in the blood vessels that contract or relax to distribute blood to the tissues in need.

The mechanism that causes contraction is the same in skeletal, cardiac, and smooth muscle. Muscles are made up of bundles of muscle cells, which are called muscle fibers. Inside each muscle fiber are hundreds to thousands of rod-like structures called **myofibrils**, which are responsible for contraction. Each myofibril is made up of even smaller structures called filaments. There are two types of filaments—thick and thin. Thick filaments are made of the protein **myosin** and thin filaments are made of long chains of the protein **actin**. In order for a muscle to contract, myosin must attach to actin and rotate, causing the thin and thick filaments to slide past each other. This sliding increases the amount of overlap of the muscle filaments and shortens the muscle. This process requires energy from ATP (Figure 3.3).

MUSCLES FOR STRENGTH, POWER, AND ENDURANCE

There are three major aspects of muscle performance: strength, power, and endurance. Muscle strength is the maximum force that a muscle can exert. Strength is directly related to muscle size; larger muscles have more strength. Power refers to how fast the muscle can develop its maximum force. It depends on both strength and speed. More muscle power gives greater acceleration, so it is important in sprint-length running and cycling events and in sports such as basketball, in which jumping is important. Increasing muscle power will increase the speed of a pitcher's fastball. Muscle endurance is the capacity to generate or sustain maximal force for an extended period of time. It is important for athletes involved in long events such as marathons, distance cycling, or triathlons.

Muscle strength, power, and endurance are due in part to the distribution of fibers within the muscles. There are two types of muscle fibers: fast twitch and slow twitch. Fast-twitch fibers can contract as much as 10 times faster than slow-twitch fibers can. **Fast-twitch fibers** have a greater capacity for ATP production via anaerobic metabolism. They are important during activities that require changes of pace or stop-and-go movement, such as basketball, soccer, and hockey. These fibers are also needed during an all-out effort requiring rapid and powerful movements, such as running a 100-meter (109-yard) dash. Having a high proportion of fast-twitch muscle fibers is an asset in time-limited activities such as sprinting, but fast-twitch fibers tire quickly.

Slow-twitch fibers develop force slowly, but can maintain contractions longer. They generate ATP primarily through aerobic metabolism. Slow-twitch fibers contain more mitochondria. Mitochondria are the power houses within cells where aerobic metabolism occurs. Slow-twitch fibers also contain more myoglobin, a protein that stores oxygen in the muscle. This makes slow-twitch fibers more efficient at using oxygen to generate ATP. If they have enough oxygen, they can stay active for a long time. The body relies on slow-twitch fibers during low-intensity endurance events, such as long bike rides, and during everyday activities, such as walking. Most activities rely on a mixture of fast-twitch and slow-twitch fibers. For example, both would play a role in relatively short, higher-intensity endurance events such as a 3.1-mile (5 kilometer) run or a quarter mile (about 400 m) swim.

Genetics largely determines a person's muscle fiber makeup. Most people tend to have an equal distribution of fast-twitch and slow-twitch fibers. However, Olympic sprinters have about 80% fast-twitch fibers, and those who excel in marathons may have

80% slow-twitch fibers. It is not clear whether training can change a person's distribution of fiber types.

THE EFFECTS OF EXERCISE TRAINING

Three things determine the availability of oxygen in muscle cells:

- How quickly the heart can pump blood from the lungs to the muscle cells
- The amount of hemoglobin in the blood, which determines how much oxygen the blood can carry
- How much oxygen can be used at the muscle cell

Training, by repeated bouts of exercise, causes physiological changes that increase the body's ability to deliver and use oxygen. Training also increases the strength and endurance of muscles

WHO HAS THE HIGHEST AEROBIC CAPACITY?

Aerobic capacity, or VO_2max, is the maximum amount of oxygen that can be taken up and used to generate ATP. Elite cross-country skiers are the most powerful athletes in terms of aerobic capacity. Because the arms are used to pull and push on the ski poles, more muscle groups are engaged in skiing than in running. Therefore, the overall energy expended in skiing is higher than the energy expended in running. Elite cross-country skiers have very high maximal oxygen uptakes; a VO_2max of 94 ml/kg/min was recorded for a male Norwegian Olympic champion cross-country skier. In contrast, competitive basketball and football players typically have VO_2max values that are about 60 ml/kg/min, healthy college-age men have VO_2max values of about 50 ml/kg/min, and poorly conditioned adults may have values below 20 ml/kg/min.

and improves the ability to dissipate heat, which enhances performance in a hot environment.

What Does Aerobic Training Do?

Aerobic exercise is performed at an intensity that increases the heart rate but still relies on aerobic metabolism. An activity is generally considered aerobic if a person can talk, but not sing, while exercising. Aerobic training causes physiological changes in the cardiovascular system and the muscles. These changes increase the aerobic capacity (VO_2max), which is the amount of oxygen that can be delivered to and used by the muscle cells. This increases overall endurance.

Regular aerobic exercise strengthens the heart muscle and increases stroke volume. When stroke volume is increased, the heart can deliver more blood with each beat. This means that the heart does not need to beat as many times to deliver enough blood to body cells at rest, and during exercise it increases the amount of oxygen that can be delivered to the muscle. Therefore, more fit people have lower resting heart rates. They can perform higher-intensity activity before reaching their maximum heart rate.

Aerobic training also causes other changes that increase aerobic capacity. It increases the number of capillaries in the muscles, so that blood is delivered to muscles more efficiently. It increases the total volume of blood and the number of red blood cells. This increases the amount of hemoglobin in the blood, which allows more oxygen to be transported at any given time. Aerobic training also causes changes at the cellular level that make it easier for muscle cells to use oxygen for energy. The number and size of muscle-cell mitochondria increase. There also is a boost in the activity of mitochondrial enzymes that are needed for aerobic metabolism and fatty acid breakdown. More fatty acids are brought to the mitochondria, and more triglycerides are stored and broken down in the muscle. These changes boost the cell's capacity to burn fatty acids to produce ATP. The use of fatty acids preserves glucose stores (glycogen), which delays the onset of fatigue. Training also makes it easier to store glucose in the muscle as **glycogen**. Because trained athletes store more glycogen and use it more slowly, they can sustain aerobic exercise for longer periods at higher intensities than untrained people can.

What Does Resistance Training Do?

Resistance training, often called strength training or weight training, involves using muscles to push against a force. Weight lifting is the most common type of resistance training. It can improve muscle strength, power, and overall endurance. Even elderly, sedentary individuals can dramatically increase muscle

HOW LOW DOES YOUR HEART GO?

What is your resting heart rate? To find out, measure your pulse when you first wake up in the morning, before your feet even hit the floor. Have a watch handy, and find your pulse. You can find it either in your wrist or at the carotid arteries in your neck. Use your index and middle fingers to count the beats. Don't use your thumb; it has a light pulse of its own that can cause confusion. If you are patient, count the number of beats in 60 seconds. Or, use a shortcut by counting the beats in 10 seconds and multiplying by 6. For example, if you count 11 beats in 10 seconds, your resting heart rate is 66.

The average resting heart rate is 66 to 72 beats per minute (bpm). A well-trained endurance athlete may have a resting heart rate of 40 bpm. Tennis great Bjorn Borg had a resting heart rate of 35 bpm. The lowest resting heart rate on record is 28 bpm, recorded for Spanish cyclist Miguel Indurain. But, resting heart rate does not necessarily predict ability and performance. Genetics has a lot to do with a person's resting heart rate. Marathon superstar Frank Shorter had a resting heart rate of 75 beats per minute. Regardless of genes, getting in better shape reduces the resting heart rate, making the heart more efficient.

strength through weight training. The body adapts to perform the task demanded, whether that task is to lift a heavier weight, stretch a millimeter farther, or continue lifting for a few minutes longer. When a muscle is exercised, the stress or overload causes the muscle to adapt by increasing in size and strength—a process referred to as **hypertrophy**. By progressively increasing the amount or intensity of exercise at each session, the muscle slowly hypertrophies. The greater the amount and intensity of exercise, the larger the effect of the training. By increasing the strength of muscles, resistance training also can improve the power of muscles. Gains in muscle endurance occur when muscle strength is increased, when cardiovascular performance is improved by aerobic training, and when diet is optimized.

When a muscle is not used, it becomes smaller and weaker. This process is called **atrophy**. If a person is bedridden and cannot move around, his or her muscles will atrophy. Once the person is up and active again, the muscles regain their strength and size.

REVIEW

ATP is needed for muscle contraction. When oxygen is present, aerobic metabolism produces ATP efficiently. In the absence of oxygen, anaerobic metabolism can produce ATP quickly, but it is less efficient. During exercise, the respiratory and cardiovascular systems work harder to deliver additional fuel and oxygen to the muscles and to remove carbon dioxide and other wastes. Cardiac output increases and the blood vessels in the muscles dilate to improve blood delivery. Muscle performance depends on strength, power, and endurance. These characteristics are due in part to the distribution of fast-twitch and slow-twitch muscle fibers. Fast-twitch fibers are better at using anaerobic metabolism. Slow-twitch fibers generate ATP primarily through aerobic metabolism. Aerobic training causes changes that increase aerobic capacity (VO_2max), which is the maximum capacity to generate ATP by aerobic metabolism. Training boosts oxygen delivery by strengthening the heart muscle and increasing stroke volume, the number of capillaries at the muscle, total blood volume, and the number of red blood cells. At the muscle, aerobic training increases the number and size of mitochondria. Resistance training, such as lifting weights, can improve muscle strength and power. When a muscle is stressed by a heavy weight, it adapts by increasing in size and strength—a process referred to as hypertrophy. In contrast, muscles that are not used get smaller and weaker, which is referred to as atrophy. Improvements in overall endurance occur when muscle strength is increased and cardiovascular performance is improved by aerobic training.

4

FOOD PROVIDES ENERGY FOR ACTIVITY

The carbohydrates, fat, and protein in food supply energy to fuel the body. Before the energy can be used, it must be converted into adenosine triphosphate (ATP). ATP can be generated with or without oxygen, depending on the duration and intensity of the exercise. The amount of oxygen at the muscles depends on the ability of the heart and lungs to deliver it.

ENERGY STORES

Energy is stored in the body in a number of forms. There are small amounts of ATP and another high-energy molecule called **creatine phosphate** stored for immediate use in the muscle. Once these are used, carbohydrates and fat stores are used to generate ATP. Protein is not stored in the body, but some body protein also is broken down to provide energy for exercise.

Carbohydrates are stored as glycogen in the muscles and liver. The amount of energy stored as glycogen is small, compared with the amount stored as fat and the amount of protein available. There are between 60 and 120 grams (equivalent to 2 to 4 ounces) of glycogen stored in the liver. Stores are highest just after a meal. Liver glycogen supplies blood glucose between meals and during the night. Eating a good breakfast will replenish the liver glycogen that was used overnight. There are about 200 to 500 grams (about ½ to 1 pound) of glycogen in the muscles of a 154-pound (70-kilogram) person. Muscle glycogen is used to fuel muscle activity. Consuming a high-carbohydrate diet can increase muscle glycogen levels.

The body's fat reserves are almost unlimited (Table 4.1). It is estimated that a 130-pound (59 kg) woman has enough energy stored as body fat to run 1,000 miles (1,609 km). Most body fat is stored as triglycerides in **adipose tissue** under the skin and around body organs. There are also small amounts of fat in muscle.

Protein used as fuel comes from the breakdown of body proteins that are less important for survival, such as muscle proteins. A considerable amount of protein can be broken down before body function is affected.

TABLE 4.1 AVAILABLE ENERGY IN THE BODY

Energy Source	Primary Location	Energy (calories)*
Glycogen	Liver and muscle	1,400
Glucose or lipid	Body fluids	100
Triglyceride	Adipose tissue	115,000
Protein	Muscle	25,000

*Values represent the approximate amounts in a 70-kg male.

HOW DOES EXERCISE DURATION AFFECT FUELS?

Which fuel powers muscles depends on how long a person has been exercising. During the first few seconds, the body can use the small amounts of ATP and creatine phosphate stored in muscles. After that, additional ATP must be made.

Energy Right Now: ATP and Creatine Phosphate

During the first few steps of a morning jog, the heart and lungs have not had time to step up oxygen delivery to the muscles. Still, ATP is needed immediately to fuel muscle contraction. During the first 10 to 15 seconds of exercise, the muscles use energy from stored ATP and creatine phosphate, another high-energy compound stored in the muscle (Figure 4.1). Oxygen is not needed to use these fuels. In a resting muscle, there is enough stored ATP to fuel muscles for about three seconds. As the ATP in muscle is used, enzymes transfer phosphate from creatine phosphate to adenosine diphosphate (ADP) to form more ATP. The amount of creatine phosphate stored in the muscle at any time is also small. It will fuel muscle activity for an additional 8 to 10 seconds.

Short, high-intensity exercise, such as a 100-meter dash, a 25-meter swim, or lifting a heavy weight, can be fueled almost exclusively by energy from stored ATP and creatine phosphate. These sources are also important in any activity requiring brief bursts of maximal effort, such as driving for a layup in a basketball game, thrusting upward during a pole vault, or launching a shot put. However, sustaining exercise beyond an immediate burst—and recovering from an all-out effort—require additional ATP. This ATP is generated from the metabolism of carbohydrates, protein, and fat.

Fueling Short-Term Exercise: Anaerobic Metabolism

After 10 to 15 seconds of exercise, the stores of ATP and creatine phosphate in muscles will be gone. However, the heart and lungs still need more time to increase oxygen delivery to the muscles. At this

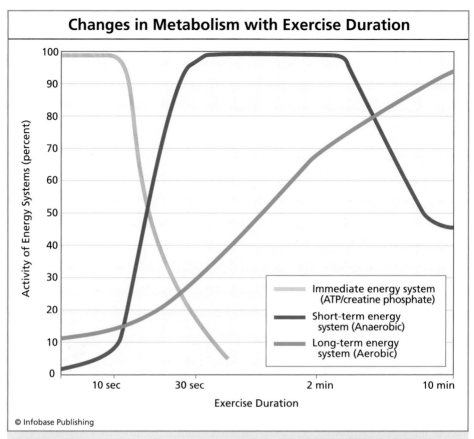

Changes in Metabolism with Exercise Duration

FIGURE 4.1 When exercise first begins, the muscles obtain energy from stored ATP and creatine phosphate. By 30 seconds into the activity, anaerobic pathways are operating at full capacity. Aerobic metabolism begins to make a significant energy contribution by about two minutes after the exercise has begun, and it is responsible for producing the energy needed for longer-term activity.

point, muscle cells use anaerobic metabolism, which does not require oxygen, to make ATP. The reactions of anaerobic metabolism take place in the cytoplasm of the cell. Anaerobic metabolism can use only glucose as fuel. In a process called glycolysist, the 6-carbon glucose is broken into two 3-carbon molecules of **pyruvate** (Figure 4.2) and generates two molecules of ATP, which are available to power muscle contraction. The byproducts of anaerobic ATP production—

Anaerobic and Aerobic ATP Production

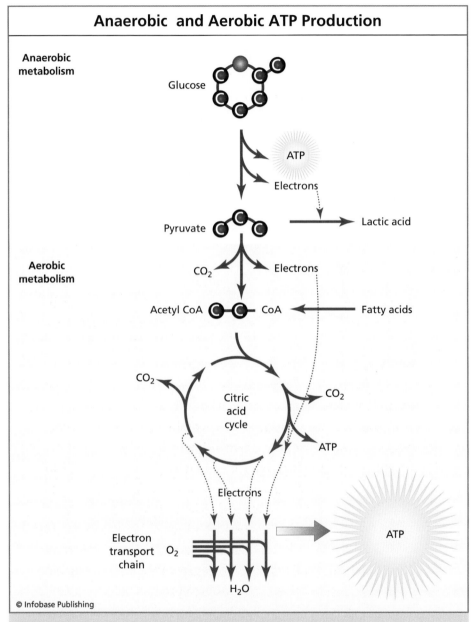

Anaerobic metabolism

Glucose

ATP

Electrons

Pyruvate → Lactic acid

Aerobic metabolism

CO_2 Electrons

Acetyl CoA — CoA ← Fatty acids

CO_2

Citric acid cycle

CO_2

ATP

Electrons

Electron transport chain O_2

ATP

H_2O

FIGURE 4.2 In the absence of oxygen, ATP is produced from glucose through anaerobic metabolism, which makes ATP quickly but inefficiently. When oxygen is available, aerobic metabolism can use both glucose and fatty acids to generate ATP. In this case, production is slower but more ATP is generated per glucose molecule.

pyruvate and high-energy electrons—combine to form a molecule called **lactic acid**. The lactic acid can be transported out of the muscle for use in other tissues. The liver can convert lactic acid back to glucose. However, if the amount of lactic acid produced exceeds the amount that can be used, it begins to build up in the muscle and the blood. This buildup of lactic acid is associated with fatigue, but is no longer believed to be an important cause of fatigue.

Energy for the Long Run: Aerobic Metabolism

After two to three minutes, heart rate and breathing rate have increased, bringing more oxygen to the muscles. Now, aerobic metabolism can begin supplying ATP. To produce ATP, aerobic metabolism can use glucose, fatty acids, and sometimes amino acids from protein. It produces ATP slower than anaerobic metabolism does, but it is much more efficient, producing about 18 times more ATP for each molecule of glucose.

The reactions of aerobic metabolism take place in cellular organelles called mitochondria. When oxygen is available, the pyruvate produced by anaerobic metabolism enters mitochondria. Here it loses a carbon atom as CO_2 combines with a molecule called coenzyme A (CoA) to form a molecule called acetyl-CoA (see Figure 4.2). When oxygen is available, pyruvate is used to make acetyl-CoA and no lactic acid is formed. The electrons released by glucose breakdown are picked up by shuttling molecules and then used to generate ATP. When fatty acids are used to produce ATP, the fatty acid chain is first broken into 2-carbon units that form acetyl-CoA. This process is called **beta-oxidation** and releases electrons that can be used to produce ATP.

Acetyl-CoA, whether produced from beta-oxidation or glucose breakdown, enters the next stage of aerobic metabolism: the **citric acid cycle**. To begin the cycle, acetyl-CoA combines with a 4-carbon molecule that comes from carbohydrate metabolism. The result is a 6-carbon molecule called citric acid. The citric acid cycle then removes one carbon at a time of CO_2 until the 4-carbon molecule is formed again. These chemical reactions produce two ATP molecules per glucose molecule. They also release high-energy electrons. The electrons are passed to shuttling molecules for transport to the last stage of aerobic metabolism, the electron transport chain.

The **electron transport chain** involves a series of molecules associated with the inner membrane of the mitochondria. These molecules accept the electrons from the shuttling molecules and pass them down the chain until they are finally combined with oxygen to form water. As the electrons are passed along, their energy is trapped and used to make ATP.

Aerobic capacity is dependent on the amount of oxygen that can be delivered to and used by the muscles. A greater aerobic capacity allows a person to perform more intense exercise without relying on anaerobic metabolism.

HOW DOES EXERCISE INTENSITY AFFECT METABOLISM?

In order to meet the energy demands of the muscles during exercise, ATP is produced by both anaerobic and aerobic metabolism.

ALTITUDE CAN AFFECT ATHLETIC SUCCESS

When people go from sea level into the mountains, they may feel lightheaded and short of breath. This is because there is less oxygen in the air at higher altitudes. This can affect athletic performance. The 1968 Summer Olympic Games were held in Mexico City, 7,349 feet (2,240 meters) above sea level. In short sprinting events, which don't depend on oxygen being available at the muscle cell, new records were set in almost every men's and women's race. However, in distance events, the thinner air took its toll. Times were slower for running events longer than about a half a mile (800 m), where having oxygen available at the muscle cells is important for ATP production. The higher altitude also had greater effects on athletes who lived at sea level than on those who were accustomed to living and exercising at high altitudes.

The amount of ATP produced by each depends on how intense the activity is. During moderate-intensity exercise, the heart and lungs can deliver enough oxygen to the muscle to support aerobic metabolism. Aerobic metabolism can use both glucose and fat to produce ATP. As exercise intensity increases, oxygen cannot be delivered to the muscle quickly enough to meet energy demands through aerobic metabolism alone, so anaerobic metabolism of glucose increases to provide additional ATP. The more intense the exercise is, the greater the proportion of ATP that is provided by anaerobic metabolism of glucose.

HOW DOES TRAINING AFFECT METABOLISM?

As was previously discussed, exercise training increases the amount of oxygen delivered to the muscles. It increases the amount of blood pumped with each heartbeat, as well as the volume of blood, the number of red blood cells, and the number of capillaries in the muscles. At the muscle cell level, exercise training increases the number and size of mitochondria, the ability to metabolize fatty acids, and the amount of stored glycogen. These physiological and biochemical effects increase a person's ability to deliver oxygen to muscle cells, and the ability of cells to produce ATP by aerobic metabolism.

Comparing the performance of a trained and an untrained person in identical tasks reveals the impact of exercise training. If two men of the same age, height, and weight were to try to ride a bicycle uphill for an hour at a set speed, the level of training would affect the type of metabolism, the fuels burned, and how long each person could continue. The trained person would be able to ride at the required speed while using predominantly aerobic metabolism. He would use mostly fatty acids as an energy source, so his glycogen stores would not be depleted. He would be able to ride for the entire hour. The untrained man would not be able to ride at the required speed using aerobic metabolism alone. He would use anaerobic metabolism of glucose to supply some of the needed energy. Before the hour was up, his glycogen stores would be empty and he would have to slow down or stop.

FUELING EXERCISE WITH CARBOHYDRATES

Glucose is the form of carbohydrate used by the muscles as a fuel source during exercise. The glucose may come from the breakdown of glycogen in the muscle, or it may be delivered by the blood. The glucose delivered by the blood comes from liver glycogen stores, glucose synthesized by the liver, and carbohydrates consumed in food or drink during exercise.

How quickly glucose is used during exercise depends on the intensity of the exercise (Figure 4.3). High-intensity exercise relies on anaerobic metabolism, which uses glucose exclusively as a source of fuel. The glucose for high-intensity exercise comes mostly from muscle glycogen. Therefore, the more intense the exercise, the more glycogen used. Muscle glycogen depletion is one factor involved in the onset of fatigue during exercise.

During low- and moderate-intensity exercise, the muscles can use fat for fuel, so glycogen is depleted more slowly. But even when aerobic metabolism predominates, some glucose still is used. Some comes from muscle glycogen and some is delivered in the blood. As muscle glycogen stores decrease, glucose delivered in the blood becomes a more important source of carbohydrates. Hormones released during exercise help ensure that blood glucose levels are maintained and can continue to supply glucose to body cells, including the muscle. For example, within seconds of the start of exercise, the hormones epinephrine and norepinephrine are released. When blood glucose levels begin to drop, the pancreas releases the hormone glucagon. These three hormones stimulate the liver to break down glycogen and make new glucose.

When liver glycogen is broken down, glucose is released into the blood. During intense or long-lasting exercise, liver glycogen can be depleted. To ensure glucose is available, glucagon also stimulates **gluconeogenesis**, or the creation of new glucose. During exercise,

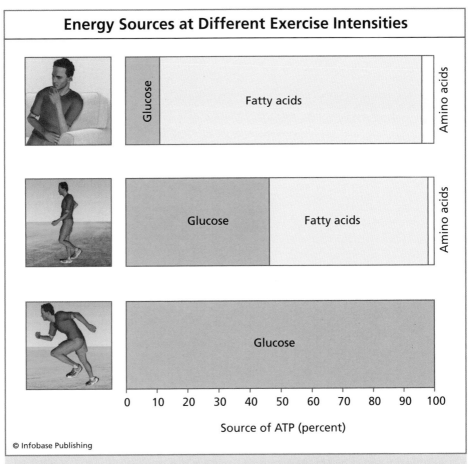

Energy Sources at Different Exercise Intensities

Glucose | Fatty acids | Amino acids

Glucose | Fatty acids | Amino acids

Glucose

0   10   20   30   40   50   60   70   80   90   100

Source of ATP (percent)

© Infobase Publishing

FIGURE 4.3 Blood flow to muscles increases dramatically during strenuous exercises, as shown by the yellow area on this graph. At rest, the muscles primarily use fatty acids as a fuel. Fatty acids are also an important fuel during moderate-intensity exercise. However, when exercise intensity is high, almost all of the energy for muscle contraction comes from glucose.

gluconeogenesis occurs primarily in the liver. It produces glucose from three-carbon molecules, including lactic acid, alanine, and glycerol. Lactic acid is generated by the anaerobic metabolism of glucose. Lactic acid produced in the muscle can travel to the liver and be converted back into glucose. Alanine is an amino acid generated from the release and breakdown of amino acids from the muscle. Glycerol is a product of triglyceride breakdown. When adipose tissue is broken down, each triglyceride molecule yields three fatty acids and a molecule of glycerol. The fatty acids are transported to the muscle. They are used to make ATP through aerobic metabolism. The glycerol goes to the liver, where it can be used for gluconeogenesis. Because beta-oxidation breaks fatty acids into two-carbon molecules, fatty acids cannot be used to synthesize glucose.

The amount of glucose that must be produced by gluconeogenesis during exercise depends on several things:

- The extent of carbohydrate stores that are present before exercise starts
- The duration and intensity of the exercise
- How much carbohydrate is consumed during exercise

During prolonged exercise (three hours or more), gluconeogenesis is a major source of glucose for muscles. Carbohydrates consumed during exercise (as drinks or snacks) can provide an additional source of glucose. This is beneficial for exercise lasting an hour or more because it will spare glycogen, reduce the need for gluconeogenesis, and delay fatigue.

FUELING EXERCISE WITH FAT

Fat is a major energy source during exercise, but it can be used only when oxygen is available. During moderate-intensity exercise (60% to 75% of VO_2max), fat is the primary energy source for muscle contraction. When fat is used as an energy source, glycogen stores are spared and exercise can continue for a longer period. A variety of dietary supplements, including carnitine and caffeine, promise to improve endurance by making it easier for the body to use fatty acids as fuel (see Chapter 8).

To be used for energy, fatty acids inside the muscle cell must be transported into the mitochondria. They are transported across the mitochondrial membrane with the help of the amino acid carnitine. Once inside the mitochondria, they are broken down to produce ATP. The rate at which the muscle can use fatty acids depends on how quickly they can be delivered to cells and then transported into the mitochondria.

Fatty acids used during exercise can come from adipose tissue, fat stored in muscle cells, fat consumed in the diet, or fat made by the liver. Most of the fat stored in the body consists of triglycerides found in adipose tissue. The breakdown of triglycerides in adipose tissue is stimulated by the rise in the hormone epinephrine that occurs as exercise begins. The resulting fatty acids are transported through the bloodstream to the muscle.

Fat stored within the muscle, referred to as intramuscular fat, can also be used as a source of energy during exercise. This fat already exists in the muscle tissue, so the fatty acids do not need to be transported in the blood. Higher-intensity aerobic exercise uses more intramuscular fat. Triglycerides consumed in the diet or made by the liver are a less important source of

THE FAT-BURNING ZONE

People who need to lose weight want to lose fat. Therefore, when they climb on a treadmill or stationary bike at the gym, they choose the workout that puts them in the "fat-burning zone", rather than the one that puts them in the "cardio zone". The fat-burning zone is a lower-intensity aerobic workout that keeps your heart rate between about 60% and 70% of maximum. The cardio zone is a higher-intensity aerobic workout that keeps heart rate between about 70% and 85% of maximum. Which workout burns more fat? The lower-intensity workout burns a higher percentage of calories from fat. But exercising in the cardio zone—for the same amount of time—burns about the same amount of fat, and more calories overall because it is more vigorous exercise. People who are tying to lose weight would therefore benefit more for the higher intensity "cardio zone" workout.

fatty acids for exercise. They are transported in the blood in particles called lipoproteins. At the muscle, an enzyme cleaves the triglycerides and allows the fatty acids to enter the muscle cell. Because people generally do not eat a large, fatty meal before exercising, the amount of energy obtained from blood lipoproteins generally is small.

WHAT IS THE ROLE OF PROTEIN DURING EXERCISE?

Although protein is not considered a major energy source for the body, the body uses small amounts of protein for energy. The amount increases in certain cases:

- If a person's diet does not provide enough total energy
- If a person consumes more protein than he or she needs
- During certain types of exercise

The amino acids available to the body come from the digestion of dietary proteins and from the breakdown of body proteins. These amino acids can be used to synthesize new body proteins or other nitrogen-containing molecules. If the nitrogen-containing amino group is removed from an amino acid, the remaining carbon compound can be broken down to produce ATP. In some cases, it can be used to make glucose via gluconeogenesis.

Protein metabolism is affected by exercise intensity. High-intensity exercise increases the rate of protein usage. Low-intensity exercise does not. Because amino acids can be used to make glucose via gluconeogenesis, protein becomes a more important energy source as carbohydrate stores are depleted. During exercise, muscles can use amino acids to generate ATP and to produce molecules needed for aerobic metabolism. After exercise, amino acids are used to build and repair muscle proteins.

The body's need for protein is increased by strength training and endurance exercise. Strength training stimulates muscle growth; additional protein is needed to supply amino acids to build muscles. Endurance exercise increases protein needs because amino acids become an important source of energy when exercise continues for many hours. Also, amino acids are used to synthesize glucose by gluconeogenesis. The glucose produced by gluconeogenesis helps maintain blood glucose levels during endurance activities. Additional protein also may be needed to repair muscle damage caused by intense training.

EXERCISE FATIGUE

Exercise fatigue is due to a combination of psychological, environmental, and physiological factors. Psychological factors, such as mood, can affect exercise performance. A depressed athlete may feel fatigued even before an athletic event. Environmental factors, such as temperature and humidity, also can affect how quickly an athlete becomes fatigued. Physiological factors that affect fatigue include changes caused by the production of heat, the buildup of metabolites from energy metabolism, and the depletion of liver and muscle glycogen. When athletes run out of glycogen, they feel overwhelming fatigue, called "hitting the wall" or "bonking." Glycogen stores are depleted faster when oxygen is not available and anaerobic metabolism predominates.

Sooner or later, all exercise causes fatigue and exhaustion. When this occurs will depend on the type and duration of exercise, the exercise intensity, and the fitness of the person exercising. During high-intensity exercise, oxygen cannot get to the muscles fast enough, so the body must rely heavily on the anaerobic metabolism of glucose. This causes glycogen stores to be used up rapidly, leading to fatigue. At a lower intensity, aerobic metabolism predominates, and exercise can continue for longer periods before fatigue sets in. Aerobic metabolism is more efficient and uses mainly fatty acids for energy, sparing glycogen. However, even aerobic metabolism uses some glucose, so glycogen stores will eventually be depleted.

REVIEW

The ATP needed to fuel the body machine is provided by carbohydrates, fat, and protein. Small amounts of ATP and creatine phosphate, another high-energy compound, are stored in muscles. Once exercise begins, these fuels are used up quickly, and additional ATP must be supplied by the breakdown of carbohydrates, fat, or protein. When oxygen is limited, as it is when exercise first begins and during intense exercise, ATP must be produced by anaerobic metabolism. Anaerobic metabolism uses only glucose as a fuel; it is a fast but inefficient way to produce ATP. It cannot sustain exercise for long periods because it quickly uses up glucose stored as glycogen. When oxygen is available at the muscles, aerobic metabolism can proceed. Aerobic metabolism can use carbohydrates, fat, or protein to produce ATP. By using fatty acids as a fuel, aerobic metabolism spares glycogen stores. Exercise that relies on aerobic metabolism can continue for a longer time period before the athlete becomes fatigued. Glycogen depletion and other changes at the muscle contribute to fatigue. Exercise training allows athletes to perform at a higher intensity before anaerobic metabolism predominates.

5

ENERGY AND NUTRIENT NEEDS OF ATHLETES

Whether marathon runners or mall walkers, people need the right nutrients. The diet must provide enough energy from the right sources to fuel activity, enough protein to maintain muscle mass, sufficient micronutrients to support energy metabolism, and enough water to transport nutrients and cool the body.

GETTING ENOUGH ENERGY

The amount of energy a person needs depends on gender, age, height, and weight, as well as activity level. This energy—measured in calories—keeps the body warm and functioning normally, maintains body tissues, and keeps muscles moving. In general, larger people need more energy than smaller ones do, younger people need more energy than older ones do, men need more energy than women do, and more active people need more energy than less active ones do.

Estimating Energy Needs

Mathematical equations have been developed for calculating energy needs. The values derived from these equations are called Estimated Energy Requirements (EERs). EERs estimate the number of calories a healthy person needs to consume to maintain their body weight. The equations take into account gender, age, height, weight, life stage, and activity level. Taller, heavier people require more energy. For example, an active 25-year-old man who is 5-foot 11-inches tall and weighs 170 pounds (about 77 kilograms) requires 3,175 calories to maintain his weight. If the same man weighed 220 pounds (100 kg), he would need about 300 calories more per day.

Separate EER equations for children, adolescents, men, women, and pregnant and lactating women reflect the differences in the energy requirements of these groups. Children and adolescents are still growing, so energy is needed for growth. Pregnant women need additional energy to allow for the growth of their own tissues and those of the fetus. Breast-feeding women need extra calories to make milk.

WHY DOES GRANDMA EAT LIKE A BIRD?

During exercise, muscles use more energy than at rest. Yet, even at rest, muscle cells require more energy than fat cells do. Because men have more muscle and less fat than women, a man requires more calories per day than does a woman of the same height and weight. The proportion of muscle versus fat also affects the amount of energy required in older versus younger adults. As adults age, the amount of muscle decreases and the amount of fat increases. This decreases energy needs. For example, the EER for an 80-year-old man is almost 600 calories less than it is for a 20-year-old man of the same size and activity level. The difference in EER between an 80-year-old woman and a 20-year-old woman of the same height, weight, and physical activity level is about 400 calories per day. Some changes in body composition can be prevented by strength-training exercise.

TABLE 5.1 LEVELS OF PHYSICAL ACTIVITY WITH PA VALUES

Physical Activity Level	PA values			
	3–18 years		≥ 19 years	
	Boys	Girls	Men	Women
Sedentary: Engages in only the activities of daily living and no moderate or vigorous activities	1.00	1.00	1.00	1.00
Low active: Daily activity equivalent to at least 30 minutes of moderate activity and a minimum of 15 to 30 minutes of vigorous activity depending on the intensity of the activity.	1.13	1.16	1.11	1.12
Active: Engages in at least 60 minutes of moderate activity or a minimum of 30 to 60 minutes of vigorous activity depending on the intensity of the activity.	1.26	1.31	1.25	1.27
Very Active: Engages in at least 2.5 hours of moderate activity or a minimum of 1 to 1.75 hours of vigorous activity depending on the intensity of the activity.	1.42	1.56	1.48	1.45

More active people need more calories to maintain their weight. The **physical activity (PA) value** is a number used in the EER calculation to account for activity level; higher numbers correspond to greater levels of activity. Activity level has a significant effect on energy needs. To determine activity level, keep an activity log for a few days. Then use Table 5.1 to determine whether you fit into the sedentary, low active, active, or very active category.

TABLE 5.2 CALCULATING ESTIMATED ENERGY REQUIREMENTS

To determine EER:

- Determine your weight in kilograms (kg) and your height in meters (m)

  Weight in kg = weight in pounds/ 2.2 pounds per kg

  Height in meters = height in inches x 0.0254 inches per m

  For example: 160 pounds (lbs) = 160 lbs/2.2 lbs/kg = 72.7 kg

  5 feet 9 inches (in) = 69 in x 0.0254 in/m = 1.75 m

- Determine your PA (physical activity) value by estimating the amount of physical activity you get per day and using Table 5.1 to find the PA value. For example, if you are a 19-year-old male who performs 40 minutes of vigorous activity a day, you are in the active category and have a PA of 1.25.

- Use the appropriate EER prediction equation below to find your EER:

  For example: if you are an active 19-year-old male,

  EER = 662 – (9.53 x age in yrs) + PA ([15.91 x weight in kg] + [539.6 x height in m])

  Where age = 19 yr, weight = 72.7 kg, height = 1.75 m, Active PA = 1.25

  EER = 662 – (9.53 x 19) + 1.25([15.91 x 72.7] + [539.6 x 1.75]) = 3,107 cal/day

Life Stage	EER Prediction Equation
Boys 9–18 yr	EER = 88.5 – (61.9 x age in yrs) + PA [(26.7 x weight in kg) + (903 x height in m)] + 25
Girls 9–18 yr	EER = 135.3 – (30.8 x age in yrs) + PA [(10.0 x weight in kg) + (934 x height in m)] + 25
Men ≥19 yr	EER = 662 – (9.53 x age in yrs) + PA [(15.91 x weight in kg) + (539.6 x height in m)]
Women ≥19 yr	EER = 354 – (6.91 x age in yrs) + PA [(9.36 x weight in kg) + (726 x height in m)]

A "sedentary" individual is someone who does not participate in any activity beyond activities such as such as housework and homework that are required for daily independent living. To be at the "low active" level, an average adult would need to do the equivalent of walking about 2 miles (3 kilometers) at a speed of 3 to 4 miles (4 to 6 km) per hour, in addition to the activities of daily living. To be "active," an individual would need to do the equivalent of walking at least 4.4 miles per day at this rate. Adults who are "very active" do the equivalent of walking at this rate for at least 10.3 miles daily. Once activity level is estimated, use the PA value to calculate EER, as shown in Table 5.2.

EXERCISE EXTREMES

The number of calories a person expends for exercise varies widely. Most people burn only a few hundred calories each day through exercise, but in extreme athletic events, such as the Tour de France, the numbers can be very high. The Tour de France is a bicycle race that lasts for three weeks. It covers more than 2,000 miles (3,220 km). The riders travel about 100 miles a day, at an average speed of about 25 miles per hour. To provide fuel for this amount of exercise, riders eat an average of 6,000 to 7,000 calories a day. On days when they ride through the Alps or Pyrenees mountains, they may need 10,000 calories. To meet these high calorie demands, athletes use a combination of liquid nutrition and normal meals and snacks. When they are not on their bikes, they eat almost continuously, but they also eat while riding. To provide for this, team cars follow the riders to supply water, sports drinks, and snacks. Sacks of snacks that riders can hang around their necks are passed out at "feeding stations" along the course. Riders try to consume 300 to 400 calories per hour while on their bikes. Despite this high caloric intake and the riders' already-low proportions of body fat, riders usually lose 4 to 7 pounds (1.8 to 3.2 kg) over the course of the event.

The Impact of Activity

Activity has a dramatic effect on calorie needs. For example, a 25-year-old man who is 71 inches (1.8 m) tall and weighs 154 pounds (70 kg) needs 2,510 calories per day. If this same man starts an exercise program to train for a marathon and runs for

TABLE 5.3 ENERGY EXPENDED FOR ACTIVITY

Activity	Energy (cal/hr)						
Body Weight (lb)	**110**	**125**	**140**	**155**	**170**	**185**	**200**
Sitting							
Male	73	77	81	85	89	93	97
Female	63	66	69	72	76	79	82
Bowling							
Male	121	128	135	142	148	155	162
Female	105	110	115	121	126	131	136
Aerobics							
Male	455	480	506	531	556	582	607
Female	394	413	433	453	472	492	511
Biking (12 mph)							
Male	380	401	422	443	464	486	507
Female	329	345	361	378	394	410	427
Walking (15 min/mi)							
Male	257	271	285	300	314	328	342
Female	222	233	244	255	266	277	288

three or four hours a week, he will need to eat more to maintain his weight. Table 5.3 illustrates how much energy is needed per hour for various activities.

The amount of energy required for an activity depends on the intensity and duration of that activity. More intense activity

Activity	Energy (cal/hr)						
Body Weight (lb)	110	125	140	155	170	185	200
Weight lifting							
Male	340	359	378	397	415	434	453
Female	294	309	323	338	352	367	382
Swimming (laps)							
Male	364	384	405	425	445	465	486
Female	315	331	346	362	378	393	409
Dancing							
Male	364	384	405	425	445	465	486
Female	315	331	346	362	378	393	409
Golf (walking with a bag)							
Male	425	448	472	496	519	543	567
Female	368	386	404	422	441	459	477
Jumping rope							
Male	595	628	661	694	727	760	793
Female	515	540	566	591	617	642	668
Running (10 min/mi)							
Male	619	653	688	722	757	791	826
Female	536	562	589	615	642	669	695

requires more calories, and the longer an activity continues, the more calories it requires. For example, running at a pace of five minutes per mile uses about 20 calories per minute. Jogging at a pace of 12 minutes per mile uses 10 calories per minute. Still, jogging at this pace for two hours will burn about 1,200 calories. Athletes that train for hours each day may need as many as 6,000 calories a day to maintain body weight.

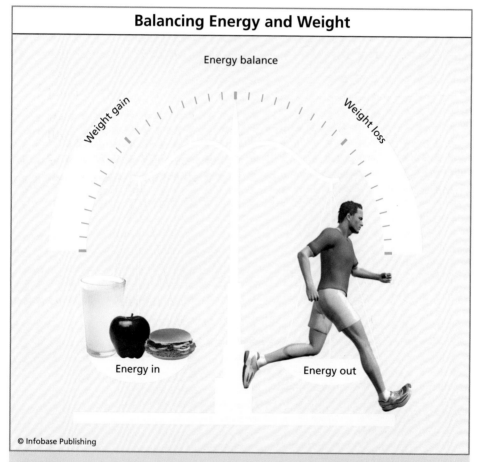

Balancing Energy and Weight

Energy balance

Weight gain

Weight loss

Energy in

Energy out

FIGURE 5.1 When the amount of energy expended by the body is equal to the amount taken in, body weight will remain stable. You can gain or lose weight by adjusting your energy intake, relative to the amount of daily activity in which you take part.

Weight Loss and Weight Gain

For weight to remain the same, a person must consume enough energy to fuel physical activity, process food, and maintain basic body functions such as breathing, circulating blood, and maintaining a constant body temperature. When the energy consumed is equal to the energy expended, body weight does not change and the body is in a state of **energy balance.** If a person does not eat enough, body fat and muscle will be used as fuel and body weight will decrease. This is good if a person is trying to lose weight, but it may not be beneficial to athletic performance. If a person takes in more calories than he or she uses, body weight will increase. If you are strength training and consume adequate protein, extra energy can be used to build muscle, which may benefit athletic performance. Yet, if muscle growth is not stimulated by weight lifting, the excess energy will be stored as body fat. How this impacts athletic performance depends on the sport. Generally, performance is optimized when athletes are in energy balance (Figure 5.1).

CARBOHYDRATE, FAT, AND PROTEIN NEEDS

Carbohydrates, fat, and protein are known as the energy-yielding nutrients. They are needed in the proper proportions to maintain ATP production during activity and prevent losses of essential body tissues.

How Much Carbohydrate Intake is Needed?

Carbohydrates are needed to provide energy and maintain blood glucose levels during exercise. They also are necessary for replacing glycogen stores after exercise. The amount of carbohydrate intake recommended for athletes depends on total energy expenditure, the type of sport, and the environmental conditions. Generally, needs range from 6 to 10 grams per kilogram of body weight per day. For a 154-pound (70 kg) person burning 3,000 calories per day, this would equal about 60% of calories from carbohydrates. Most carbohydrates in the diet should be complex carbohydrates from whole grains and starchy vegetables, with some naturally occurring simple sugars found in fruit and milk. Before or during competition, however, low-fiber snacks are best because they leave the stomach quickly. A full stomach during exercise can cause cramping and gastrointestinal distress.

How Much Fat?

Fat is an important source of energy for exercise. It also provides essential fatty acids and is necessary for the absorption of fat-soluble vitamins. Body stores of fat provide enough energy to support the needs of even the longest endurance events. For physically active people, diets providing 20% to 25% of calories as fat are recommended. Because fat leaves the stomach slowly, high-fat foods should be avoided before or during exercise. This will reduce the chances of cramps and gastrointestinal distress.

WHICH BAR IS BEST?

Looking for a snack that will fit in a bike pack or pocket? A sports bar would be perfect, but deciding which one may be challenging. There are many types, and they vary in nutrient composition and in the promises they make. For an energy boost during a bike ride or day of skiing, try a high-carbohydrate bar, often called an energy or endurance bar. These have the carbohydrates needed to prevent hunger and maintain blood glucose during a sporting event. But are they any healthier than candy bars? Typically, they are lower in fat, higher in fiber, and contain more vitamins and minerals than candy bars do. They are probably not as good as a meal, but they fit in a pocket easier than a peanut butter sandwich and a banana.

FIGURE 5.2 Many athletes believe protein is the key to building muscle mass and strength. People who are trying to increase their muscle mass or improve their performance will often turn to supplements or powders to increase their protein intake.

How Much Protein?

Protein accounts for only about 5% to 10% of energy used, but it plays a critical role in the health and performance of athletes. Protein is needed to maintain and repair lean tissues, including muscle. But muscle growth is stimulated by exercise, not by eating more protein. A diet that contains the Recommended Dietary Allowance for protein (0.8 grams per kilogram of body weight) provides enough protein for most active people.

Competitive athletes who participate in endurance and strength sports may need more protein. In endurance events, such as marathons, protein is used for energy and to maintain blood glucose. To provide for this, endurance athletes may need to consume 1.2 to 1.4 g of protein/kg per day. Strength athletes who need amino acids to make new muscle proteins may benefit from 1.2 to 1.7 g of protein/kg per day. This amount may seem like a lot, but it is not much more than what is in the diets of typical American athletes. For example, a 187-pound (85-kg) man who consumes the typical American diet with 3,000 calories and 135 grams of protein per day would be consuming 1.6 g of protein/kg of body weight. If the diet is adequate in energy, the recommended amount of dietary protein can easily be consumed without supplements (Figure 5.2).

VITAMIN AND MINERAL NEEDS

Getting enough vitamins and minerals is crucial to athletic performance. They help produce ATP, deliver oxygen, repair and maintain the body, and protect the body from oxidative damage.

The B vitamins thiamin, riboflavin, niacin, vitamin B_6, pantothenic acid, and biotin are particularly important for the production of ATP from carbohydrates and fats. Vitamin B_6, folate, and vitamin B_{12} are B vitamins that are used to make new red blood cells. Vitamin B_6 is needed to make hemoglobin, the protein red blood cells use to carry oxygen. Folate and vitamin B_{12} are needed for cell division.

The minerals calcium, iron, and zinc also have important roles in exercise. Calcium is needed to build and repair bones. It is also essential for muscle contraction and the transmission of nerve signals. Iron is a necessary part of hemoglobin as well as myoglobin, a protein that increases the amount of oxygen available to the muscle. A number of iron-containing proteins also are needed for production of ATP by aerobic metabolism. Zinc plays a role in the growth, synthesis, and repair of muscle tissue, as well as energy metabolism. Athletes do not need more of these minerals than non-athletes do. However, athletes' diets—particularly those of female athletes—often are deficient in these minerals.

Vitamins and minerals with antioxidant functions also are important during exercise. Exercise increases the rate of chemical reactions that produce ATP. These reactions generate dangerous oxygen compounds that can cause oxidative damage to tissues. Antioxidants, such as vitamins C and E, beta-carotene, and selenium, protect the body from oxidative damage. Despite this, research does not show that athletes need more antioxidant nutrients than non-athletes do or that antioxidant supplements improve athletic performance.

Do athletes need more vitamins and minerals? Exercise stresses many metabolic pathways that require these nutrients, increases loss of vitamins and minerals from the body, and increases the amounts of vitamins and minerals needed for repair and maintenance. In most cases, however, a diet that provides the recommended amounts of vitamins and minerals will meet the needs of athletes. In addition, because energy needs are increased by activity, athletes eat more food. Along with this food will come more vitamins and minerals. Athletes who consume low-fat diets, restrict their intake of energy or specific food groups, or have limited intakes of fruits and vegetables may be at risk for vitamin or mineral deficiencies.

WATER NEEDS

Water also is an essential nutrient. The amount of water needed depends on the person and the type and location of the exercise they are performing. In general, the water needs of athletes are higher than those of non-athletes. Maintaining water balance is crucial to successful exercise (see Chapter 6).

REVIEW

Athletes require more calories than non-athletes do. The estimated energy requirements (EERs) can be used to calculate energy needs. If energy intake is equal to energy use, the athlete will maintain a constant body weight. An athlete's diet should provide enough carbohydrates to maintain blood glucose levels during exercise and replace glycogen stores after exercise. Fat is an important source of energy during exercise, but the diet should be fairly low in fat to allow enough carbohydrates to be consumed. Only small amounts of protein are used to provide energy during exercise, but protein is important for muscle maintenance and repair. Although certain vitamins and minerals have particularly important roles that support exercise, a diet that provides the amounts recommended by the DRIs will still meet an athlete's needs. Water needs generally are higher in athletes than in non-athletes.

6

KEEPING COOL: WHY ARE WATER AND ELECTROLYTES SO IMPORTANT?

About 60% of body weight is water. The human body contains more water than any other nutrient, including protein or fat. A person probably could live for eight weeks without food, but without sufficient water, he or she could survive for only three to four days. Because water cannot be stored, the amount of water taken into the body must be balanced with water losses to maintain homeostasis. Exercise increases the loss of water and electrolytes. If they are not replaced, the resulting imbalance can impair exercise performance and compromise health.

WATER AND ELECTROLYTES IN YOUR BODY

Water is found in all the tissues of the body. Some is found inside cells, where it is known as **intracellular fluid**. **Extracellular fluid** is found outside cells. About one-third of the water in the body is extracellular fluid. Most of it is fluid between cells, called **interstitial fluid**, and the rest is water found in blood **plasma, lymph,** and the gastrointestinal tract, eyes, joints, and spinal cord.

Electrolytes in Body Water

Body water contains dissolved substances, including sodium, potassium, and chloride. These negatively and positively charged **ions** are referred to as **electrolytes** because they conduct an electrical current when dissolved in water. There are other electrolytes in body fluids, but the term commonly refers to these three because they are the most abundant. Most sodium and chloride is found in extracellular fluids, and most potassium is found inside cells. Electrolytes help regulate the distribution of water throughout the body.

Water Moves by Osmosis

Water can move freely across cell membranes. **Osmosis** is the movement of water across a membrane from an area with a low concentration of dissolved substances to an area with a high concentration of dissolved substances. Therefore, it is the concentrations of dissolved substances (such as sodium, chloride, and potassium, as well as magnesium, calcium, and many other molecules) that determine the distribution of water. For example, if the concentration of sodium in the blood is high, water from the interstitial fluid is drawn into the blood, diluting the sodium (Figure 6.1). Electrolytes help maintain fluid balance within the body by helping to keep water within a particular compartment. Electrolyte concentration is also important in regulating the total amount of body water. As

FIGURE 6.1 When the concentration of solvents in the fluid surround cell is greater than the concentration inside the cells, water will move out of the cells, causing them to shrink. This same process occurs when you sprinkle sugar on strawberries (*left*). The sugar dissolves in the moisture on the surface of the strawberries and osmosis causes water to move out of the strawberries to dilute the sugar. The strawberries get smaller and softer.

a result, adequate water intake and electrolyte balance are both important for proper fluid balance during exercise.

WHAT DOES WATER DO?

Water has many functions in the body. It transports nutrients and other substances. It provides structure and protection. It is needed for numerous chemical reactions. Water also is important for the regulation of body temperature.

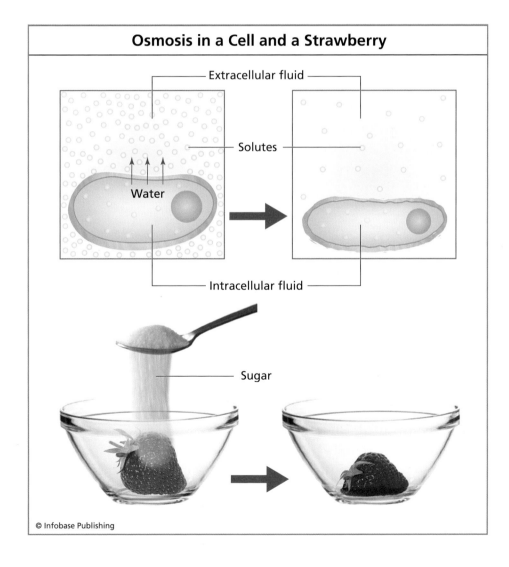

Osmosis in a Cell and a Strawberry

Extracellular fluid

Solutes

Water

Intracellular fluid

Sugar

© Infobase Publishing

Water Transports Substances

Water bathes the cells of the body and serves as a transport medium to deliver substances to cells and remove wastes. Blood is 90% water. Blood transports oxygen, nutrients, hormones, immune factors, drugs, and other substances to cells. It then carries carbon dioxide and other waste products away from the cells for elimination from the body. During exercise, the need for oxygen and nutrients at the muscle cells increases, as does the production of wastes. Therefore, the need for water as a transport medium is even more crucial during exercise.

Water Provides Structure and Protection

Water is a part of the structure of a number of molecules, including glycogen and proteins. It also makes up most of the volume of body cells. Muscle is about 75% water and bone is 25% water. Adipose tissue, where fat is stored, is 20% to 35% water. Water helps protect the body by serving as a lubricant and cleanser. Watery tears moisten the eyes and wash away dirt. Saliva keeps the mouth moist, making it easier to chew and swallow food. Water also protects the body by acting as a cushion. For example, fluids inside the eyeballs and spinal cord act as cushions against shock, and the fluid in our joints cushions and lubricates them during movement.

Water Is Needed for Chemical Reactions

Water is involved in numerous chemical reactions throughout the body. It is the medium for all metabolic reactions. Water is an ideal solvent because the two ends of the water molecule have different electrical charges: One end is positive and one end is negative. This property allows water to surround other charged molecules and disperse them. For example, table salt consists of a positively charged sodium ion and a negatively charged chloride ion. When placed in water, the sodium and chloride ions move apart, because the sodium ion is attracted to the negative end of the water molecule and the chloride ion is attracted to the positive end.

Water also participates directly in a number of chemical reactions, many of which are involved in energy metabolism. The addition of water to a large molecule can break it into two smaller ones. Likewise, the removal of a water molecule can join two molecules. Water helps maintain the proper level of acidity in the body. Acid balance is regulated by chemical reactions in body fluids, gas exchange at the lungs, and the filtration and elimination of certain substances by the kidneys. Water plays an important role in each of these. Acid balance is particularly important during exercise.

Water Regulates Body Temperature

Exercise generates heat. This occurs because the efficiency of converting the chemical energy in ATP into the mechanical energy of muscle contraction is between 20% and 25%. The other 75% to 80% of energy is lost as heat. In addition, the chemical reactions of aerobic and anaerobic metabolism also generate heat. For exercise to continue, the body must dissipate this heat. There are a number of ways in which water helps to eliminate heat during exercise.

The water in blood helps regulate body temperature by increasing or decreasing the amount of heat lost at the body surface. When body temperature starts to rise, the blood vessels in the skin become wider, or dilate. This increases blood flow to the skin. When blood is close to the surface of the body, it can release some of the heat into the environment. This is why light skin reddens in hot weather or during strenuous activity. In a cold environment, the opposite occurs. The blood vessels in the skin constrict, reducing the flow of blood near the surface and conserving heat.

The most obvious way that water helps regulate body temperature is through sweating. When body temperature increases, the brain triggers the sweat glands in the skin to produce sweat, which is mostly water. Heat is lost as the sweat evaporates from the surface of the skin. This cools the body.

WATER INTAKE

Water in the diet comes mostly from beverages (including water itself), but also from solid food (Table 6.1). Low-fat milk is 90% water, apples are about 85% water, and meat is about 50% water. A

TABLE 6.1 AMOUNT OF WATER IN FOODS

Food	Ounces (grams) of water	Percent water by weight
Orange, 1 medium	4 oz (114 g)	87
Grapes, 1 cup	4.5 oz (129 g)	81
Carrots, 1 cup	4 oz (108 g)	88
Broccoli, 1 cup	3 oz (81 g)	89
Spaghetti, cooked, 1 cup	3 oz (87 g)	62
Whole wheat bread, 2 slices	0.7 oz (19 g)	38
Low-fat yogurt, 1 cup	7 oz (208 g)	85
Ice cream, 1 cup	3 oz (88 g)	61
Chicken breast, roasted, 3 ounces	2 oz (55 g)	65
Egg, 1 hard boiled	1 oz (37 g)	74

small amount of water is generated inside the body through metabolism, but this is not significant in meeting the body's water needs.

Water is absorbed from the gastrointestinal tract by osmosis. The volume of water and the concentration of nutrients consumed with the water influence the rate of absorption. Consuming a large volume of water increases its rate of absorption. Water consumed alone will easily move from the intestine into the blood, where the concentration of dissolved substances (solutes) is higher. Absorption is slower when water is consumed with meals, because the digestion of nutrients from the meal increases the concentration of dissolved substances in the intestine. As the nutrients are absorbed and move into the blood, the concentration of dissolved substances in the intestine decreases. Water then moves by osmosis into the blood (toward the area with the highest solute concentration).

About 7 cups (1.7 liters) of water enter the GI tract each day from the diet. Another 29.5 cups (7 L) come from saliva and other gastrointestinal secretions. Most of this fluid is absorbed in the small intestine, and a smaller amount is absorbed in the colon.

WATER LOSSES

Water is lost from the body in urine, feces, and sweat, as well as through evaporation from the lungs and skin. A typical young man loses about 15.5 cups (3.7 L) of water daily. He loses more if he is sweating from exercise or the heat.

Average urine output is about 4.2 to 8.4 cups (1 to 2 L) per day, but this varies depending on the amount of fluid consumed and the amount of waste to be excreted. The waste products that must be excreted in urine include **urea** and other nitrogen-containing products from protein breakdown, ketones from fat breakdown, phosphates, sulfates, electrolytes, and other minerals.

DIARRHEA CAN BE DEADLY

Diarrhea kills about 2 million children around the world every year. The diarrhea is usually caused by a bacterial or viral infection. Diarrhea depletes the body of water and electrolytes. The resulting dehydration, when severe, can cause collapse of the blood circulation, resulting in death. Children are more likely than adults to die from diarrhea because they become dehydrated more quickly. When a child has diarrhea, the lost fluid must be replaced. Plain water is not the best choice, because it replaces only the water and not the electrolytes. Mixtures of sugar, electrolytes, and water called Oral Rehydration Solutions (ORS) replace the lost water and electrolytes in the right proportions. The sugar contained in ORS enables the intestine to absorb the fluid and electrolytes more efficiently. Treatment with ORS is effective for about 95% of people suffering from acute watery diarrhea. The World Health Organization adopted ORS as its primary tool to fight diarrhea in 1978. Since then, the mortality rate for children suffering from acute diarrhea has been cut by more than half.

The amount of urea that must be excreted increases with more dietary protein intake or body protein breakdown. **Ketone** excretion is increased when body fat is broken down, such as during weight loss. The amount of sodium that must be excreted goes up when more is consumed in the diet. In all of these cases, the body needs more water in order to produce more urine to excrete the extra wastes.

The amount of water lost in the feces is only about one-half to one cup (100 to 200 mL) per day. This is remarkable, because every day about 38 cups (9 L) of fluid enter the gastrointestinal tract from food, beverages, and gastrointestinal secretions. Under normal conditions, more than 95% of this fluid is reabsorbed before the feces are eliminated. However, in cases of severe diarrhea, large amounts of water can be lost.

Water loss due to evaporation from the skin and respiratory tract takes place continuously. These losses are referred to as insensible losses because people are not aware that they are happening. An inactive person at room temperature loses a little over 4 cups (1 L) of water per day through insensible losses, but the amount varies depending on body size, environmental temperature and humidity, and physical activity. For example, more water is lost when the humidity is low, such as in the desert, than it would be on a rainy day.

Water also is lost in sweat. The amount of water lost this way depends on environmental conditions (temperature, humidity, wind speed, radiant heat), clothing, exercise intensity, level of physical training, and the degree to which the exerciser is acclimated to his or her environment. Sweat rate increases as exercise intensity builds and as the environment becomes hotter and more humid. An individual doing light work at a temperature of about 84°F (29°C) will lose about 8.5 to 12.5 cups (2 to 3 L) of sweat per day. Strenuous exercise in a hot environment can cause water losses in sweat to be as high as 8.5 to 17 cups (2 to 4 L) in one hour. Clothing that allows sweat to evaporate will help keep the body cool and will decrease sweat losses. Athletes who are more highly trained sweat more, not less, as conventional wisdom might indicate. Those accustomed to a hot environment also sweat more.

A cold environment also can increase the amount of water lost from the body. Cold air is less humid, so more water is lost through evaporation from the respiratory tract. Cold temperatures stimulate an increase in urine production, increasing water loss. Dissipating the heat produced while exercising in a cold environment can be difficult because of clothing. People often overdress, so as exercise proceeds, the excess heat produced cannot be transferred to the environment.

Altitude is another factor that may increase water loss from the body. Altitudes higher than 8,200 feet (2,500 meters) increase urinary losses and evaporative losses from the respiratory tract, and decrease appetite. The increase in urine output lasts for about seven days and increases water loss by about 2 cups (500 ml) per day. Due to the dry air at high altitudes, respiratory water losses may be as high as 8 cups (1,900 ml) per day in men and 3.6 cups (850 ml) per day in women. The decrease in appetite that occurs at high altitude makes it more difficult to drink to replace water losses. Fluid intake per day at high altitude should be increased to as much as 13 to 17 cups (3 to 4 L) per day.

WATER AND ELECTROLYTE BALANCE

To maintain water and electrolyte balance, intake and excretion must balance. Water intake is stimulated by thirst, but is not finely regulated this way. Water loss is more closely regulated by the kidneys, which can increase or decrease urinary losses. The kidneys also regulate electrolyte losses in the urine over a wide range of intakes, making electrolyte imbalances unlikely in healthy people.

Thirst

The need to consume water or other fluids is signaled by the sensation of thirst. Thirst is triggered both by sensations in the mouth and signals from the brain. When a person needs water, the mouth becomes dry because less water is available to produce saliva. When body water levels drop, the thirst center in the brain senses a decrease in the amount of water in blood and an increase in the concentration of dissolved substances in the blood. The feeling of a dry mouth and signals from the brain cause the sensation of thirst and motivate a person to drink.

Thirst is not a perfect regulator of water intake. Thirst is quenched almost as soon as fluid is consumed and long before body water balance has been restored. Also, the sensation of thirst often lags behind the actual need for water. For example, athletes exercising in hot weather lose water rapidly, but they do not experience intense thirst until they have lost so much body water that their physical performance is compromised. Also, thirsty people cannot and do not always respond to thirst. To prevent dehydration, the kidneys regulate water loss more closely.

Kidneys Regulate Water and Electrolyte Excretion

The kidneys serve as a filtering system that regulates the amount of water and dissolved substances retained in the blood and excreted in urine. As blood flows through the kidneys, water and small molecules are filtered out. Some are reabsorbed and the rest are excreted in the urine. The amount of water and electrolytes that are reabsorbed depends on conditions in the body. Two hormonal systems regulate fluid and electrolyte balance.

One system responds to changes in the concentration of solutes in the blood (Figure 6.2). When the concentration is high, the pituitary gland secretes **antidiuretic hormone (ADH)**. This hormone signals the kidneys to reabsorb water, reducing the amount lost in the urine. The reabsorbed water is then returned to the blood, preventing the solute concentration from increasing further. When the solute concentration in the blood is low, ADH levels decrease, so less water is reabsorbed and more is excreted in the urine.

The other system is activated by changes in blood pressure and relies on the ability of the kidneys to conserve sodium. Because water follows sodium by osmosis, changes in the amount of sodium retained or excreted result in changes in the amount of body water.

When the concentration of sodium in the blood decreases, water moves out of the blood, decreasing blood volume. This decreases blood pressure. When this happens, the kidneys release an enzyme called renin. **Renin** begins a series of events that lead to the production of **angiotensin II**. Angiotensin II increases blood pressure

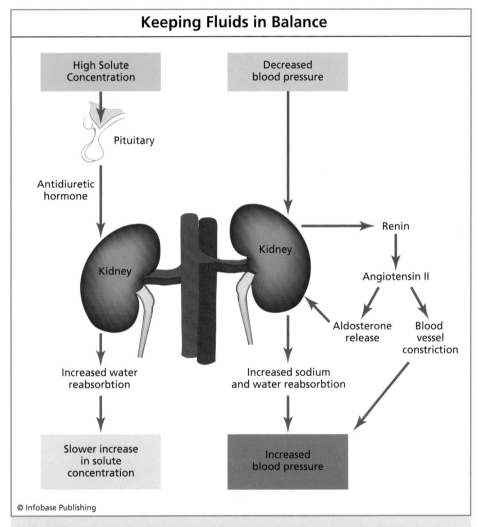

Keeping Fluids in Balance

High Solute Concentration

Decreased blood pressure

Pituitary

Antidiuretic hormone

Renin

Kidney

Angiotensin II

Kidney

Aldosterone release

Blood vessel constriction

Increased water reabsorbtion

Increased sodium and water reabsorbtion

Slower increase in solute concentration

Increased blood pressure

© Infobase Publishing

FIGURE 6.2 Fluid balance is regulated by antidiuretic hormone and the renin-angiotensin system, which triggers the release of the hormone aldosterone. When the body senses changes in its overall water level, it uses these systems to keep its fluids in balance.

in two ways. One is by causing blood vessel walls to constrict and the other is by stimulating the release of the hormone **aldosterone**, which acts on the kidneys to increase the amount of sodium reabsorbed into the blood. Water follows the reabsorbed sodium, and is returned to the blood. As blood pressure returns to normal, the release of renin and aldosterone are inhibited. This keeps blood pressure from continuing to rise.

The kidneys also regulate potassium excretion. The long-term regulation of potassium balance, like that of sodium, depends on aldosterone release, which causes the kidney to excrete potassium and retain sodium.

PROBLEMS WITH FLUID AND ELECTROLYTE BALANCE

During exercise, most people only drink enough to keep them from being thirsty. By the time they finish exercising, they are dehydrated, and must restore fluid balance during the hours after exercise. Even when endurance athletes consume fluids at regular intervals throughout exercise, they often cannot take in enough to make up for losses from sweat and evaporation through the lungs. Electrolytes also are lost in sweat. The amounts lost are usually small, but if the volume of sweat is great, these losses—particularly of sodium—can add up and affect health.

Dehydration

Dehydration results when water losses exceed water intake. Dehydration hastens fatigue and makes exercise seem more difficult. Dehydration severe enough to cause clinical symptoms can occur more rapidly than any other nutrient deficiency. Likewise, health can be restored in a matter of minutes or hours if fluid is replaced.

Early symptoms of dehydration include headache, fatigue, loss of appetite, dry eyes and mouth, and dark-colored urine (Figure 6.3). Even mild dehydration—a body water loss of 2% to about 3% of body weight—can impair physical and cognitive performance. A 3% reduction in body weight can significantly reduce cardiac

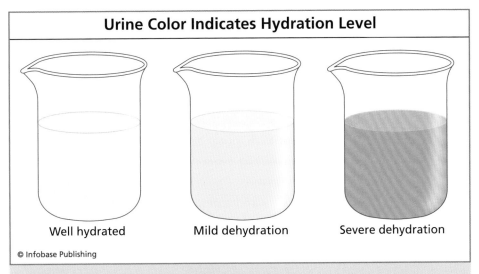

Urine Color Indicates Hydration Level

Well hydrated   Mild dehydration   Severe dehydration

© Infobase Publishing

FIGURE 6.3 If the body is not well hydrated, the kidneys excrete less water in the urine. Dehydration causes urine to become more concentrated and, as a result, a darker shade.

output; even if the heart beats much faster, it cannot make up for the decrease in stroke volume. When less blood is pumped, the ability to deliver oxygen and nutrients to cells (and remove wastes) is reduced. The lowered blood volume reduces sweat production and blood flow to the skin, as well. This limits how well the body can cool itself. If core body temperature increases, the athlete is at risk for **heat-related illnesses**.

As water losses increase, more water is lost from intracellular spaces. This water is needed to maintain metabolic functions. A loss of 5% body weight as water can cause nausea and difficulty concentrating. When water loss approaches 7% of body weight, confusion and disorientation may occur. A loss of about 10% to 20% can result in death.

Heat-Related Illnesses

During exercise, heat production increases along with exercise intensity. If heat cannot be released from the body, body temperature rises and exercise performance (as well as health) may be jeopardized. How well a body gets rid of heat generated during exercise depends upon hydration status and the conditioning of the exerciser, as well as environmental conditions. Dehydration dramatically increases the risk of heat-related illness; exercise conditioning lowers the risk. The effects of environmental conditions depend on both temperature and humidity. As temperature rises, it becomes more difficult for the body to dissipate heat. As humidity rises, it is more difficult to cool the body by evaporation. **Apparent temperature,** or **heat index**, is a measure of how hot it feels. The heat index depends on relative humidity and temperature. For example, when the humidity is 100%, a temperature of 82°F (28°C) feels the same as a temperature of 90°F (32°C) and a humidity level of 50%. The risks associated with exercising under these conditions are similar.

Heat-related illnesses include heat cramps, heat exhaustion, and heat stroke. Heat cramps are involuntary muscle spasms that occur during or after intense exercise, most often in the muscles that were used. They are caused by an imbalance of sodium and potassium at the muscle cell membranes.

Heat exhaustion occurs when fluid loss causes blood volume to decrease so much that it is not possible to both cool the body and deliver oxygen to active muscles. Heat exhaustion is characterized by a rapid, weak pulse; low blood pressure; fainting; profuse sweating; and disorientation. Someone experiencing heat exhaustion symptoms should stop exercising immediately and move to a cooler environment. If exercise continues, heat exhaustion may progress to heat stroke.

Heatstroke, the most serious form of heat-related illness, occurs when the temperature regulatory center of the brain fails due to a very high core body temperature (greater than 105°F, or 40°C). Heatstroke is characterized by extreme confusion, unconsciousness, and hot, dry skin. It requires immediate medical attention.

Children have a larger surface-to-volume ratio than adults do, which allows them to dissipate heat from the skin more efficiently. Even with this advantage, they are at a greater risk than adults are for heat-related illness because they produce more heat, are less able to transfer heat from muscles to the skin, and sweat less than

DIARRHEA CAN BE DEADLY

The first women's Olympic marathon was run in 1984, under the hot California sun. The winner was American Joan Benoit, but the most dramatic finish belonged to Swiss marathoner Gabriela Andersen-Scheiss. When she entered the Olympic stadium to run the final 400 meters of the race, she was staggering as if she were drunk. Her left arm hung limp at her side and her right leg was stiff. It wasn't clear whether she could negotiate the final lap around the track to complete the marathon. Medical officers rushed over to help her, but she waved them off. By carefully observing her condition, doctors made the decision to allow her to continue unaided. The physicians could see that although

(continues)

FIGURE 6.4 At the 1984 Los Angeles Olympics, Swiss marathon runner Gabriela Andersen-Scheiss entered the Olympic stadium and managed to stagger the last 400 meters (1,312 feet) to the finish line. She was carried off the track and treated for heat exhaustion.

(continued)

she was seriously dehydrated, she was still sweating. This suggested that she was not yet suffering from heat stroke, the most severe and life-threatening form of heat-related illness. Her final lap around the track to the finish line took 5 minutes and 44 seconds. Medics immediately treated her for heat exhaustion. She recovered rapidly and was released from the hospital after only two hours to return to the Olympic village for dinner. Her struggle to finish earned her 37th place and demonstrated that heat and dehydration can have devastating effects on health and performance.

adults do. To reduce risks, children should rest periodically in the shade, consume fluids frequently, and limit the intensity and duration of activities on hot days. Younger people also may take longer to acclimate to heat, so they should exercise at a reduced intensity and take more time to get used to their conditions than adult competitors would need.

Low Sodium: Hyponatremia

Sweat is important for cooling the body. Sweat is mostly water. For most activities, sweat losses can be replaced with ordinary water. However, sweat also contains some minerals—primarily sodium and chloride, with a smaller amount of potassium—and during prolonged exercise, the loss of sodium through sweat can be great enough to affect health and performance. A reduction in the level of sodium in the blood is referred to as **hyponatremia**. This condition can occur if an athlete loses large amounts of water and salt in sweat and then tries to replace the loss with water alone. This dilutes the sodium in the blood. It is something like dumping out half of a glass of salt water and replacing what was poured out with plain water. Athletes can lose 2 to 3 grams of salt per liter of sweat. It is not unusual for an athlete to lose a liter (4 cups) of sweat per hour, so he or she may sweat away 20 or more grams of salt during a 10-hour

FIGURE 6.5 Korey Stringer, an offensive lineman for the Minnesota Vikings, died from heatstroke in 2001 after training outdoors for more than two and a half hours. When he reached the hospital, his internal temperature was 108°F (42°C) and he was experiencing major organ failure.

competition. It is also possible to develop hyponatremia even when salt losses from sweating are not excessive. This can occur if an athlete drinks too much water, which dilutes the sodium in the system. For example, an athlete may overhydrate while exercising in a cooler climate, where sweat losses are lower. It is the concentration of sodium that is important, not the absolute amount.

Hyponatremia causes a number of problems. Sodium in the blood helps hold fluid in the blood vessels. As sodium concentration drops, fluid will leave the bloodstream by osmosis. It builds up in the tissues, causing swelling. In the lungs, fluid accumulation interferes with the exchange of oxygen and carbon dioxide. In the brain, excess fluid causes disorientation, seizure, coma, and even death. The early symptoms of hyponatremia may be similar to those of dehydration: nausea, muscle cramps, disorientation, slurred speech, and confusion. But drinking water will make the problem worse and can lead to seizure, coma, or death.

Hyponatremia is a serious concern in endurance events that take place in hot environments. About 30% of the finishers of the Hawaii Ironman Triathlon are both hyponatremic and dehydrated. Mild symptoms of hyponatremia can be treated by eating salty foods or drinking a sodium-containing beverage, such as a sports drink. People with more severe symptoms need medical attention. Athletes can reduce the risk of hyponatremia by using sodium-containing sports drinks during long-distance events and increasing their sodium intake several days prior to competition. Athletes also should avoid Tylenol, aspirin, ibuprofen, and other nonsteroidal anti-inflammatory agents. These drugs interfere with kidney function and may increase the risk of hyponatremia.

WATER AND ELECTROLYTE NEEDS

On an average day, adult men need about 15.6 cups (3.7 L) of water and women about 11.4 cups (2.7 L). People get this water from drinking water itself, as well as consuming other fluids and foods. Water and other beverages account for about 80% of fluid intake. The other 20% comes from foods. Beverages that contain caf-

TABLE 6.2 RECOMMENDED FLUID INTAKE FOR EXERCISE

Before Exercise
- Drink generous amounts of fluid in the 24 hours before exercise.
- Drink about 2 cups of fluid four hours before exercise.

During Exercise
- Drink at least 6 to 12 ounces of fluid every 15 to 20 minutes.
- For exercise lasting 60 minutes or less, plain water is sufficient for fluid replacement.
- For exercise lasting longer than 60 minutes, a sports drink may improve endurance and protect health.

After Exercise
- Begin replacing fluids immediately after exercise.
- Drink 16 to 24 ounces of fluid for each pound of weight lost.

feine do provide water, but caffeine is a diuretic: a substance that increases water loss in the urine. In general, caffeine-containing beverages only increase water loss for a short time. Over the course of a day, then, they do contribute to fluid needs. However, they are not a good drink choice during exercise.

People who exercise require extra fluids. Water is the only fluid most people need, but sports drinks are fine, too. They are not harmful and may offer some benefits. How a beverage affects fluid balance depends on the composition of the beverage consumed, the rate at which it is ingested, how quickly it leaves the stomach, and how fast it is absorbed from the intestines. A good sports drink should empty from the stomach rapidly, enhance intestinal absorption, and promote fluid retention. To ensure hydration, adequate fluids should be consumed before, during, and after exercise (Table 6.2).

What and How Much Should You Drink During Exercise?

During exercise, people should try to drink enough to balance water loss. Thirst is not a good indicator of fluid need, so exercisers should schedule fluid breaks. Even with regular fluid intake, it can be difficult to stay hydrated. People can sweat faster than they can absorb new fluid. In most cases, however, the amount of fluid ingested by the athlete does not exceed the amount that can be absorbed and is enough to balance fluid losses. An exerciser's best bet to stay hydrated is to drink 6 to 12 ounces (177 to 355 ml) of fluid every 15 to 20 minutes, beginning at the start of exercise.

Intense exercise that lasts longer than an hour may deplete the body's carbohydrates stores. A beverage containing 4 to 8 grams of carbohydrates per 100 milliliter of water can help. Popular sports drinks, such as Gatorade and Powerade, have this level of carbohydrates. These beverages are also fine to drink during shorter bouts of exercise, though they are not necessary. The carbohydrates help maintain blood glucose levels, providing a source of glucose for the muscles and delaying fatigue. Drinks with higher amounts of carbohydrates will empty from the stomach more slowly, delaying absorption. These types of drinks, such as fruit juices and soft drinks, are not recommended unless they are diluted with an equal volume of water.

Sodium and other minerals are lost in sweat. This loss usually does not affect health or performance if the exercise lasts less than about three hours. However, a beverage containing 0.5 to 0.7 grams

MAKE YOUR OWN SPORTS DRINK

Sports drinks consist of water, sugar, and salt. People can save some money by making their own. Mix 4 teaspoons of sugar and ¼ teaspoon salt in 1 cup of water. Then add flavoring, such as a teaspoon of lemon juice.

of sodium per liter (1.2 to 1.8 grams of sodium chloride per liter) is recommended for people exercising one hour or more. Even in exercise lasting less than three hours the sodium is beneficial because it makes the drink taste better and can stimulate thirst; this can help increase fluid intake. Some sports drinks contain this much sodium, but others do not. A drink containing sodium also will help prevent hyponatremia in athletes who overhydrate and in those participating in endurance events, such as ultramarathons or Ironman triathlons, who lose large amounts of sodium in sweat.

What and How Much Should You Drink After Exercise?

During exercise, people usually drink one-third to two-thirds of the water they lose in sweat. At the end of the exercise session, they are dehydrated. After exercising, to restore water balance, people should drink 16 to 24 ounces (0.5 to 0.7 L) of fluid for each pound of weight lost during exercise. Drinking a sodium-containing beverage, or drinking water and eating a food that contains sodium, is recommended. This will cause less water to be lost in the urine, compared with drinking plain water. The sodium also will help maintain the proper concentration of sodium in the blood. This will sustain the desire to drink.

If athletes gain—rather than lose—weight during exercise it indicates that they have consumed more fluid than they lost. This puts them at risk of hyponatremia.

REVIEW

Water is essential for survival. In the body, water transports nutrients and other substances and provides structure and protection. It is needed for numerous chemical reactions and helps regulate body temperature. Water is found in intracellular and extracellular compartments, and moves between them by osmosis. Water cannot be stored, so for a person to stay hydrated, intake must equal output. Water is consumed in beverages and food, and small amounts are produced in the body by metabolism. Water is excreted in urine and feces and is lost in sweat and through evaporation from the skin and lungs. Water balance is regulated primarily by the kidneys. If body water is low, antidiuretic hormone causes a reduction in urine output and other hormones cause the kidney to retain sodium. These actions increase water retention. A reduction in body water can have dire consequences for health. Mild dehydration can result in headache, fatigue, loss of appetite, and dark urine. More severe dehydration can affect the circulatory system and the body's ability to cool itself. Dehydration can be fatal. It also can lead to other heat-related illnesses, such as heat cramps, heat exhaustion, and heat stroke. To prevent these problems, athletes should be well hydrated before they exercise. During exercise, athletes should try to drink enough fluid to replace losses. For exercise lasting more than an hour, fluids containing sugar and electrolytes are recommended. During prolonged exercise, replacement of fluids with plain water can dilute blood sodium and cause hyponatremia. After exercise, fluid losses can be replaced by drinking 16 to 24 ounces (0.5 to 0.7 L) of water for every pound of weight lost.

7

WHAT SHOULD ATHLETES EAT?

For most people who exercise, a balanced and healthy diet is enough. For competitive athletes, however, the right food choices can mean the difference between victory and defeat.

WHAT SHOULD ATHLETES EAT?

The recommendations for a healthy diet apply to athletes as well as non-athletes. When planning an athlete's diet, MyPyramid is a good place to start. However, if athletes train for many hours each day, their energy needs exceed those recommended for even the most active exercise category included in MyPyramid. To provide the extra calories, the amounts from each food group should be increased above the recommendations for people at the very active physical activity level. Athletes involved in heavy training may need to eat more than six times per day to meet their energy needs.

Although the overall diet of an athlete does not need to be different from anyone else's, the timing of meals and foods relative

113

to workouts and competitions, as well as the composition of these meals and foods, need to be considered. An athlete's response to particular foods and meals is also an important concern when planning what to eat before, during, and after an exercise session.

MAXIMIZING STORED GLYCOGEN

Consuming enough carbohydrates to maintain glycogen stores is important for all athletes. Glycogen provides a readily available source of stored glucose. Larger glycogen stores allow exercise to continue longer. Consuming a high-carbohydrate diet can increase glycogen stores, and hence increase endurance (Figure

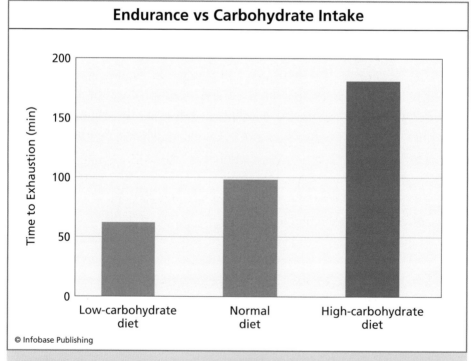

FIGURE 7.1 Consuming a high-carbohydrate diet increases the level of glycogen, or stored energy, in muscles, allowing people to exercise for longer periods. This graph illustrates the impact of carbohydrate intake on cycling endurance.

7.1). Following a regimen called **glycogen supercompensation**, or **carbohydrate loading**, can maximize glycogen stores. This regimen involves resting for one to three days before competition while consuming a diet very high in carbohydrates. The diet should provide 10 to 12 grams of carbohydrates per 2.2 pounds (1 kilograms) of body weight, or about 700 grams per day for a 154-pound (70-kg) person. Three cups of spaghetti with garlic bread provides only about 20% of this amount. Because consuming this much carbohydrates can be difficult, there are a number of high-carbohydrate beverages available that contain 50 to 60 grams of carbohydrates per cup. These should not be confused with sports drinks designed to be consumed during competition, which contain only about 15 to 20 grams of carbohydrates per cup. In a trained athlete, a glycogen supercompensation regimen can double the amount of muscle glycogen.

Although glycogen supercompensation is beneficial to endurance athletes, it will provide no benefit for those who exercise for periods shorter than 60 minutes. It actually has some disadvantages at this level of exercise. For every gram of glycogen deposited in the muscle, almost 3 grams of water are also deposited. This water will cause weight gain and may cause muscle stiffness. As the glycogen is used, the water is released. Although this can be an advantage when exercising in hot weather, the extra weight may cancel any potential benefits from increased stores, especially for short-duration events.

THE PRE-EXERCISE MEAL: WHAT TO EAT BEFORE COMPETITION

Most people don't perform at their best when hungry. Athletes perform better after eating a small meal than they do when they are in a fasting state. The size, composition, and timing of a pre-exercise meal are important. The wrong meal can hinder performance more than the right one can enhance it.

Meals eaten before competition or workouts should maintain hydration, prevent hunger, and fill energy stores, while minimizing gastric distress. About 2 cups of fluid should be consumed to ensure that the athlete is adequately hydrated. Meals should be high in carbohydrates (60% to 70% of calories) to maintain blood glucose and glycogen stores. Muscle glycogen is used up only by exercise. However, liver glycogen supplies glucose to the blood and is depleted even at rest if no food is eaten. A high-carbohydrate meal, consumed two to four hours before an event, will fill liver glycogen stores. This meal should also be low in fat (10% to 25% of calories) and fiber to minimize gastrointestinal distress. It should be moderate in protein (10% to 20% of calories), and should consist of foods that are familiar to the athlete. A pancake breakfast or a plate of pasta with marinara sauce would be good choices. Spicy foods should be avoided, because they may cause heartburn.

DON'T GO SWIMMING ON A FULL STOMACH

As children, some people were told not to go in the water for a half an hour after eating. The theory is that digestion increases blood flow to the stomach. If a person starts to swim, the muscles also need blood, and the body can't send enough blood to both places. Reduced blood flow to the muscles could lead to cramps, which increases the risk of drowning. Swimming competitively on a full stomach could lead to cramps and possibly vomiting, but for most recreational swimmers, the chance of cramps is small. The chances of drowning due to cramps are even smaller. The American Red Cross does not recommend waiting any amount of time after eating before taking a swim. While it is an old wives's tale, it may hold more than a grain of truth if the meal includes an alcoholic beverage. Up to half of adolescent and adult deaths associated with water recreation are related to alcohol use. So have lunch and enjoy a swim, but stay out of the water if the poolside indulgence involves alcohol.

Large amounts of simple sugars also should be avoided, because they could cause diarrhea.

In addition to providing nutritional benefits, a meal that includes "lucky" foods may provide some athletes with a psychological advantage. Because foods affect people differently, athletes should test the effects of meals and snacks during training, not during competition.

WHAT TO EAT ON THE RUN

Fluid consumption is essential during all types of exercise, but for exercise that lasts more than an hour, carbohydrate consumption also can be beneficial. An intake of 0.7 grams of carbohydrate per kilogram of body weight per hour, or about 30 grams to 60 grams per hour, helps maintain blood glucose and enhance performance. This is equivalent to drinking 2.5 cups (0.6 L) of Gatorade per hour, or eating a banana and an energy bar. Consuming carbohydrates probably won't help if exercise lasts an hour or less, but it probably won't hurt, either. Current research supports consuming carbohydrates in the amounts contained in most sports drinks (6% to 8%). This is particularly important for athletes who exercise in the morning, when liver glycogen levels are low.

Carbohydrate intake should start shortly after exercise begins. Consume regular amounts every 15 to 20 minutes. The carbohydrate should be glucose, glucose polymers (chains of glucose molecules), or a combination of glucose and fructose. Fructose alone is not absorbed as quickly and may cause diarrhea. The carbohydrate can be provided by sports drinks, solid food, or energy gels. Gels come in small packets. They consist of a thick carbohydrate syrup or paste. Each packet provides between 17 grams and 25 grams of carbohydrate.

During exercise, sodium and other minerals are lost through sweat. The amounts lost during exercise lasting less than about three hours usually will not affect health or performance. However, a sodium-containing snack or beverage is recommended for exercise lasting more than an hour. Sodium makes beverages taste better and increases the drive to drink, so consuming it during exercise may help athletes drink more and stay hydrated.

POST-EXERCISE MEALS

When exercise ends, the body must shift from breaking down glycogen, triglycerides, and muscle proteins for fuel to rebuilding glycogen stores, depositing lipids, and synthesizing muscle proteins. Foods and beverages consumed after exercise must provide enough fluid and electrolytes to replace losses, carbohydrates to restore glycogen, and protein to build and repair muscle tissue.

The first priority is to replace lost fluids. A beverage other than plain water also can help replace electrolytes. Whether a person needs food immediately and what he or she should eat depends on how long and how intense the exercise session was, and when

DON'T FORGET THE FLUIDS!

Some endurance athletes do not like to eat during competition, but consuming carbohydrates is essential if they want to continue high-intensity exercise. To avoid eating solid foods, many athletes have begun to use energy gels as a source of carbohydrates. A gel comes in a foil packet that can be easily opened and the contents squeezed into the mouth. Each packet typically contains 17 grams to 25 grams of carbohydrate; consuming one or two packs each hour provides enough carbohydrate to maintain the body's supplies. Gels are easy to carry, easy on the stomach, and don't cause bloating. However, gels do not provide fluid. Without sufficient fluid, carbohydrate absorption is slowed and performance is affected. To stay hydrated, and absorb the carbohydrates efficiently, athletes should drink about 8 ounces of water with each packet.

the next session will occur. If glycogen was not depleted, food may not be needed until the athlete feels hungry. If it was depleted, the time of the next exercise session determines how fast it needs to be replenished to ensure maximum performance.

When timed properly, post-exercise carbohydrate intake can replenish muscle and liver glycogen stores within 24 hours of the athletic event. The body is most efficient at replenishing glycogen stores during the first hour after exercise. So to maximize replacement, an athlete should consume a high-carbohydrate meal or drink within 30 minutes of completing the athletic event, and consume another one every two hours after that, for six hours. Ideally, the drinks or meals should provide 1.0 to 1.5 grams of carbohydrate per kilogram of body weight, which is about 70 to 100 grams of carbohydrate for a 154-pound (70-kg) person—the equivalent of two pancakes with syrup and a glass of fruit punch. The type of carbohydrate also affects glycogen synthesis. Glucose and sucrose are equally effective, but fructose alone is less effective.

This type of regimen to restore glycogen is critical for athletes who have to perform again the next day. This schedule is not necessary if the athlete has one or more days to replace glycogen stores before the next intense exercise session. In that case, carbohydrates can be provided over a 24-hour period, and the timing of intake does not matter. Even if a person is going to exercise the next day, timed glycogen replacement may not be necessary. For example, if a person's typical exercise session is a 30-minute to 60-minute workout at the gym, he or she does not need timed replacement. A typical diet providing about 55% of calories from carbohydrates will replace the glycogen used, and the body will be ready to work out again the next day.

REVIEW

The timing, amounts, and types of food eaten before, during, and after workouts and competitions can affect exercise performance. To load muscle glycogen stores to the maximum, endurance athletes can follow a regimen called glycogen supercompensation. However, this may be a disadvantage for short events. A pre-exercise meal consumed two to four hours before athletic competition can maximize energy stores and minimize gastrointestinal distress during an event. The ideal meal provides enough fluid to ensure adequate hydration, is high in carbohydrates to supply blood glucose and fill glycogen stores, and is low in fat and fiber, to avoid abdominal distress. During exercise, it is important to replace lost fluids and, for exercise lasting more than an hour, the consumption of carbohydrates and sodium, along with fluid, is recommended. After competition, food and drink should be consumed to replace fluid, electrolyte, and glycogen losses and provide enough protein for muscle repair. After exercise, if carbohydrate intake is done at the right times, muscle and liver glycogen stores can be replenished within 24 hours of the athletic event.

8

ERGOGENIC SUPPLEMENTS: ARE THEY SAFE?

For as long as there have been athletic competitions, athletes have longed for and experimented with anything that might provide a competitive edge. Everything from desiccated liver to shark's cartilage has been used in the hopes of enhancing athletic performance. Most of these **ergogenic aids** provide more of a psychological than a physiological edge. Some can enhance performance in certain types of activities and some have no effect, but others can impair health and performance.

Anything designed to enhance performance can be considered an ergogenic aid. Running shoes, drugs, and even counseling by a sports psychologist can be considered ergogenic aids. Special diets and dietary supplements also are used as ergogenic aids. Many supplements are expensive, and most have not been shown to improve performance. Yet the desire to be the best may cause athletes to ignore the potential hazards of a supplement and believe the unbelievable.

WEIGHING THE RISKS AND BENEFITS

Anyone who wants to use an ergogenic supplement should weigh the health risks against potential benefits. Just because a product is sold doesn't make it safe. Just because something appears in print does not mean it is true. Choosing to use an ergogenic aid is a serious decision. Before using a product, discuss it with your doctor. Many supplements can have dangerous interactions with other drugs. They also can make existing health conditions worse. Other things to consider:

- Are the product's claims valid?
- Is the recommended dose safe?
- Is it ethical to take the supplement?

Are the Supplement Claims Valid?

To determine if claims made about an ergogenic supplement are reliable, look beyond the marketing materials (Table 8.1). Don't trust one source of information. Look for more articles or the opinion of experts in the field of nutrition and exercise. Does the claim make sense? If it sounds too good to be true, it probably is. For example, products that claim to bring about quick improvements, such as an increase in muscle strength over only a day or two, should be viewed skeptically. Products that claim to contain a secret ingredient or formula also are suspicious. Scientific information and medical advances are published, shared, and scrutinized—they would not be kept secret. Another clue that a product may not be all that it promises is the use of popular TV personalities or star athletes as spokespersons in advertisements. This strategy encourages people to believe that if they use the product, they will look or perform like the spokesperson. The person who promotes a product has no impact on how effective or safe it is.

Where did the claim come from? Is it from an article in a scientific journal? Is it in a magazine, newspaper, or book? Is it from a company selling a product? Research studies published in reputable scientific journals are the most reliable source of information. Be aware, however, that one research study is never final proof. Several well-done studies are needed to establish the effectiveness of a substance, and completing such studies may take years. However, the results of a new study may look too good

ARE YOU SURE YOUR SUPPLEMENT IS SAFE?

Dietary supplements, including those taken to enhance athletic performance, are not regulated like drugs are. The U.S. Food and Drug Administration (FDA) does not need to approve supplements before they are sold, and manufacturers do not have to prove a product's safety and effectiveness before it is marketed. Dietary supplement manufacturers are expected to follow certain "good manufacturing practices" to ensure that products are processed consistently and meet quality standards. Once dietary supplements are on the market, the FDA does monitor them for safety. If the FDA finds a product to be unsafe, it can take action against the manufacturer, issue a warning, or require that the product be removed from the marketplace.

The FDA does regulate the information that appears on supplement labels and in package inserts. But this information can be misleading. For example, a manufacturer can say that a dietary supplement will alleviate a nutrient deficiency, support health, or is linked to a particular body function (such as immune function or protein synthesis) because the statements describe the normal role of the nutrient. The claim that a supplement "supports muscle growth" simply means that the ingredients in the supplement are needed to synthesize new muscle tissue. It does not mean that taking the supplement will make your muscles grow. This type of claim can be identified because it must be followed by the words, "This statement has not been evaluated by the Food and Drug Administration. This product is not intended to diagnose, treat, cure, or prevent any disease." The Federal Trade Commission (FTC) regulates product advertising; it requires that all information be truthful and not misleading. However, the information in magazines and brochures about nutritional ergogenic aids is not regulated. It may be exaggerated or inaccurate.

TABLE 8.1 TIPS FOR EVALUATING NUTRITIONAL CLAIMS

- **Is it reasonable?** Does the information presented make sense?
  If not, disregard it.
- **Who's making the claim?** Where did the information come from? If it is based on personal opinions, be aware that one person's perception does not make something true.
- **Who stands to benefit?** Is the information helping to sell a product? Is it making a magazine cover or newspaper headline more appealing? If so, the claims may be exaggerated to help make a sale.
- **Is it based on sound science?** If a statement claims to be based on a scientific study, think about who did the study, what their credentials are, and what relationship they have to the product.
- **What are the risks?** Be sure the expected benefit of the product is worth any risks associated with using it.

to wait for validation, and an article in a magazine or newspaper may be based on a single new scientific study. Articles in magazines and newspapers may be reliable. But they also are written to sell magazines. Claims may be exaggerated to make a magazine cover or newspaper headline more appealing.

Looking at the credentials of the person who wrote the article also can help. Articles written by people with nutrition or sports medicine degrees, or by registered dietitians, are usually reliable.

Is the Product Safe at the Recommended Dose?

Many nutritional supplements are safe at low doses but have adverse effects at high doses. The dose recommended to improve performance may have side effects that outweigh any benefits. For example, large amounts of caffeine have an ergogenic effect, but in many people, this dose causes intestinal cramps that impair performance. The length of time over which the product must be taken also should be considered. Some ergogenic aids must be used continuously to have an effect, but may be unsafe in the long run. Others are so new that no one yet knows what the long-term effects will be.

Is Taking the Supplement Legal and Ethical?

The ancient Greek ideal and the ideal of the International Olympic Committee is that an athlete should triumph through his or her own unaided effort. Everyone must assess his or her own ethical standards, but should also take into consideration:

- The policy of the team
- Whether the substance is banned from use during competition
- Whether taking it is cheating or giving an unfair advantage

Legal considerations are another factor. Professional and amateur sports organizations now have strict regulations on what supplements are considered legal and what kind of testing will be done to assure compliance with these regulations.

WHY DO WE COMPETE?

The word *compete* is derived from the Latin word *competere*, which means "to strive together." Is this still true in modern sporting events? Today, the word *competition* is more likely to mean rivalry. The dangerous overuse of supplements, legal and not, suggest that winning, by *any* means possible, is the goal.

ARE VITAMIN SUPPLEMENTS ERGOGENIC?

Vitamins don't provide any energy, but they are needed for the body to use the energy in carbohydrates, fats, and protein. This is one reason why many vitamin supplements are marketed to athletes as ergogenic aids. For example, thiamin, riboflavin, niacin, pantothenic acid, and vitamin B_6 are marketed as ergogenic aids because they are involved in muscle energy metabolism. Thiamin and pantothenic acid are needed for carbohydrates to enter the citric acid cycle for aerobic metabolism. Riboflavin and niacin are needed to shuttle electrons to the electron transport chain so ATP can be formed. Vitamin B_6 is needed to use amino acids for energy, to break down muscle glycogen, and to convert lactic acid to glucose in the liver. Supplements of vitamins B_6, B_{12}, and folic acid are promoted for athletes because they are needed to transport oxygen to exercising muscle—vitamin B_6 because it is needed for the synthesis of hemoglobin, and folic acid and vitamin B_{12} because they are both involved in the replication of red blood cells. Although a deficiency of one or more of these vitamins would interfere with energy metabolism and impair athletic performance, consuming more than the recommended amounts as supplements has not been shown to enhance performance.

Supplements of vitamin E, vitamin C, and beta-carotene are marketed to athletes due to their antioxidant functions. Exercise increases oxygen use and oxidative processes, which boosts the production of free radicals. **Free radicals** are reactive chemical substances that can damage tissues. They also have been associated with fatigue during exercise. It has been suggested that antioxidant supplements prevent free radical damage and delay fatigue, but research examining the effect of exercise on the need for antioxidants has not demonstrated that athletes require more antioxidants than nonathletes.

Although vitamin supplements may not give an athlete the winning edge, there is little risk as long as consumption does not exceed Tolerable Upper Intake Levels (ULs). (See Appendix for more details.)

ARE MINERAL SUPPLEMENTS ERGOGENIC?

Minerals like chromium and iron sound tough as nails. Supplements of these and other minerals promise to make people stronger, faster, or able to continue longer. Some of the minerals promoted as performance enhancers include chromium, vanadium, selenium, zinc, and iron. As with vitamin supplements, many of the claims made about these minerals are based on their physiological functions.

Chromium supplements, in the **chromium picolinate** form, are claimed to increase lean body mass and decrease body fat. Chromium is needed for insulin to function at its best. One of the actions of insulin is to promote protein synthesis. Therefore, getting enough chromium is likely to be important for making muscle protein. The picolinate form is absorbed better than other forms of chromium. Unfortunately, studies in humans have not consistently demonstrated an effect of supplemental chromium picolinate on muscle strength, body composition, body weight, or other aspects of health. A UL has not been established for chromium.

Vanadium, usually sold in the form of vanadyl sulfate, is another mineral marketed for its ability to assist insulin. Vanadium supplements are promised to increase lean body mass, but there is no evidence that they do. Toxicity is a concern. A UL of 1.8 mg per day of elemental vanadium has been set for people who are age 19 or older.

Selenium is marketed for its antioxidant properties and zinc for its role in protein synthesis and tissue repair. Neither of these supplements has been found to improve athletic performance in people who are not deficient in these minerals. Iron is marketed as an ergogenic mineral because it is needed for hemoglobin synthesis. If a person is iron deficient, hemoglobin cannot be made in sufficient amounts. This limits the transport of oxygen and impairs exercise performance. Iron deficiency is common in female athletes. Iron supplements can be of benefit in cases of iron deficiency.

DO PROTEIN SUPPLEMENTS STIMULATE MUSCLE GROWTH?

There are hundreds of protein powders and bars. They are typically marketed with the promise that they will increase muscle size and strength and decrease recovery time. Muscle growth does require additional protein, but protein isn't automatically deposited in muscles. Muscle growth occurs in response to exercise in the presence of adequate protein. The protein provided by expensive supplements will not meet an athlete's needs any better than the protein found in a balanced diet. Strength athletes and endurance athletes need more protein than the general population, but they can still get enough through diet. A typical diet in the United States provides about 90 grams of protein. This is almost twice the RDA for an adult. Because athletes consume more calories, they will also consume more protein with those calories.

Protein supplements are not harmful for most people, but they are an expensive and unnecessary way to increase protein intake. Protein is needed for proper immune function, healthy hair, and muscle growth, but a protein supplement will improve these parameters only if a person's diet is deficient in protein in the first place. Increasing protein intake above the RDA does not provide greater protection from disease, make hair shinier, or stimulate muscle growth. In fact, a high intake of protein may contribute to dehydration, and could actually hurt athletic performance. Muscles use carbohydrates for fuel. If too much is replaced by protein, muscle and liver glycogen stores will be low, which will compromise endurance.

ARE AMINO ACID SUPPLEMENTS ERGOGENIC?

Some amino acid supplements are marketed with claims to boost the body's natural production of hormones that stimulate protein synthesis. For example, the amino acids ornithine, arginine, and lysine are marketed with the promise that they will stimulate the release of growth hormone and, in turn, enhance the growth of muscles. Large doses of these amino acids do increase the release of growth hormone. Yet, in athletes taking these amino acids at the recommended dose, growth hormone levels are no higher than levels resulting from exercise alone. Thus, supplementation has not been found to increase muscle mass and strength any more than strength training alone.

Amino acid supplements also are marketed for a number of other reasons. Glycine supplements are promoted because glycine is a precursor to creatine (discussed below). However, glycine does not provide the ergogenic effects that creatine supplements do. Glutamine supplements supposedly increase muscle glycogen deposition following intense exercise, enhance immune function, and prevent the adverse effects of overtraining (such as fatigue and increased incidence of certain infections). Research has not supported these claims. Glutamine has not been found to increase glycogen synthesis. Glutamine is important for immune system cells, and decreases in plasma glutamine have been reported following prolonged exercise. However, studies have not consistently shown that glutamine supplements improve immune system function or help reduce the effects of overtraining.

The branched-chain amino acids (leucine, isoleucine, and valine) are the predominant amino acids used for fuel during exercise. Supplements of these are promoted to improve performance in endurance athletes. But studies have shown that they do not enhance performance, particularly when compared to the endurance-enhancing effect of carbohydrate supplementation.

There is little evidence to support the use of amino acid supplements by athletes. In general, these supplements are not recommended. High doses of individual amino acids may interfere with the absorption of other amino acids from the diet. There also have been several reports of illness caused by contaminants in the supplements.

DOES CREATINE GIVE YOU QUICK ENERGY?

Want more quick energy? To get it, many athletes experiment with creatine supplements. **Creatine** is a nitrogen-containing compound found in the body, primarily in muscle, where it is used to make creatine phosphate. Creatine phosphate is a high-energy molecule that can convert ADP to ATP to provide energy for short bursts of activity (Figure 8.1). The kidneys, liver, pancreas, and other tissues all make creatine. It also is consumed in the diet in meat and milk. The more creatine in the diet, the more the muscles will store. Supplements of creatine claim to increase the amount of creatine and creatine phosphate in the muscle;

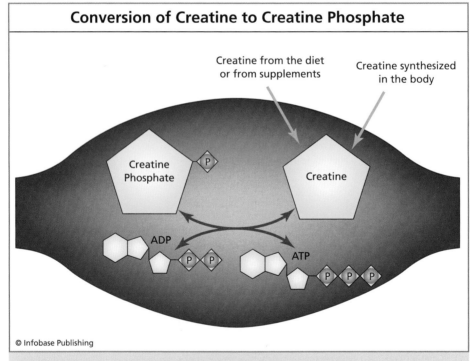

Conversion of Creatine to Creatine Phosphate

Creatine from the diet or from supplements

Creatine synthesized in the body

Creatine Phosphate

P

Creatine

ADP

P P

ATP

P P P

© Infobase Publishing

FIGURE 8.1 The more creatine consumed, the greater the amount stored in the muscle and converted to creatine phosphate. When you need energy the creatine phosphate can give its phosphate to ADP to form ATP, which can power your muscles.

increase short-duration, high-power performance; increase muscle mass; and delay fatigue.

Research shows that creatine supplements do increase the levels of creatine and creatine phosphate in muscle. This gives muscles more quick energy for activity, delays fatigue, and prevents the buildup of lactic acid. It also allows creatine phosphate to be regenerated more quickly after exercise. Creatine supplementation helps for exercise that requires explosive bursts of energy that last 30 seconds or less, such as sprinting and weight lifting. Creatine supplements also increase muscle mass. This may occur because when muscles take up more creatine, they also retain more water. An increase in muscle mass and strength also may occur because athletes taking creatine supplements can train more intensely, and for longer periods of time. Creatine is not useful for long-term endurance activities, such as marathons.

A number of studies have suggested that creatine supplements are safe, but controlled toxicology studies have not been done. No one knows how safe and effective creatine supplements are over the long term. Product purity also is a concern. Because 1 to 6 teaspoons (5 to 30 g) of creatine is needed to be effective, even a minor contaminant might be consumed in significant amounts. Ingestion of creatine before or during exercise is not recommended, and the FDA has advised consumers to consult a physician before using creatine.

DOES BICARBONATE BOOST HIGH-INTENSITY ACTIVITY?

If an athlete exercises at a high intensity, his or her body must use anaerobic metabolism to meet the demand for ATP. Anaerobic metabolism produces lactic acid. Acid in the muscle could affect muscle function and lead to fatigue. Preventing acid buildup might improve performance and delay fatigue.

Bicarbonate ions act as buffers in the body. Buffers prevent changes in acidity. Some have suggested that **bicarbonate** supplementation will neutralize the acids that build up during anaerobic metabolism. Taking sodium bicarbonate—better known as baking soda—before exercise has been shown to improve performance and delay exhaustion in sports that involve intense

WHAT CAUSES AN ENERGY DRINK'S BOOST?

Energy drinks with names like Amp, Monster, Hype, and Full Throttle are growing in popularity. They promise to give an energy boost that lasts all day. But the ingredient that gives the boost is nothing new: caffeine. Some believe caffeine use may date back to the Stone Age. This white, bitter-tasting, crystalline substance was first isolated from coffee in 1820. Today, it is the world's most popular drug. Caffeine is found naturally in coffee beans, tea leaves, cocoa beans, and cola nuts. It is added to carbonated beverages, non-prescription medication, and "energy supplements."

Caffeine stimulates the brain and affects behavior. Consuming 75 to 150 milligrams of caffeine elevates activity in many parts of the brain. It also postpones fatigue and enhances performance at both intellectual tasks and physical work that involves endurance. The amount of caffeine that food products, such as soda, can contain is limited by the Food and Drug Administration (for example, about 70 mg of caffeine for a 12-oz can). But energy drinks are considered dietary supplements, so caffeine content is not regulated. Thus, manufacturers of energy drinks can load their products with caffeine. Coffee beverages also may contain more because the caffeine is present naturally. Though people the world over start their day with a cup of caffeine, too much can be dangerous. Caffeine intoxication is a recognized clinical syndrome that causes nervousness, anxiety, restlessness, insomnia, gastrointestinal upset, tremors, rapid heartbeat, restlessness, and in rare cases, death. Table 8.2 compares the caffeine content of different types of coffee, tea, energy drinks, and other foods and beverages.

exercise lasting only a few minutes. However, it is of no benefit for lower-intensity aerobic exercise. Many people experience abdominal cramps and diarrhea after taking sodium bicarbonate. Other possible side effects have not been carefully researched.

TABLE 8.2: CAFFEINE CONTENT

Beverage or food	Caffeine (mg)
Coffee and tea drinks	
Starbucks™ coffee, grande (16 oz)	330
Starbucks™ latte or cappuccino, grande (16 oz)	150
Regular Coffee (7 oz)	80–175
Espresso (1.5 oz)	100
Decaf coffee, brewed (7 oz)	3–4
Tea, brewed (7 oz)	40–60
Soda	
Mountain Dew™ (regular or diet, 12 oz)	55
Cola (regular or diet, 12 oz)	40–46
7-Up™ (regular or diet, 12 oz)	0
Energy Drinks	
Jolt™ Cola (12 oz)	100
Red Bull (8 oz)	80
5-Hour Energy (2 oz)	138
Rockstar energy shot (2.5 oz)	200
Monster (16 oz)	160
Chocolate	
Hershey™ Bar (1.55 oz)	11
Dark Dove™ Chocolate (1.5 oz)	23
Medications	
Excedrin™ (2 caplets)	130
Vivarin™ (2 caplets)	400

CAFFEINE: COFFEE TO GO LONGER AND FARTHER

Will drinking a cup of coffee help a person run farther? Caffeine is a stimulant. It is found in coffee and many soft drinks. It is used as an ergogenic aid because it enhances the release of fatty acids. When fatty acids are used as a fuel source, glycogen is spared. This delays the onset of fatigue. Research shows that caffeine can enhance an athlete's performance during prolonged, moderate-intensity endurance exercise, as well as short-term, intense exercise. One cup of coffee is not enough, but drinking 2.5 cups of coffee up to an hour before exercising does improve endurance. Not everyone will benefit, however. Athletes who are not used to caffeine consumption will respond better than those who consume it every day. Caffeine may upset some athlete's stomachs. It also is a diuretic, but it is not likely to increase the risk of dehydration during exercise.

Whether or not caffeine is effective, it is illegal to consume excess caffeine to enhance performance during athletic competition. The International Olympic Committee prohibits athletes from competing when urine caffeine levels are 12 µg per ml or greater. For urine caffeine to reach this level, an individual would need to drink 6 to 8 cups of coffee within about two hours. Caffeine is also found in pill form in products such as NoDoz™, which contains about 100 mg of caffeine per tablet—about the same amount as in a cup of coffee.

DOES CARNITINE HELP BURN FAT?

If fat could get into muscle mitochondria faster, ATP would be produced more efficiently, glycogen would be spared, and endurance would increase. The manufacturers of **carnitine** supplements claim that this is what these supplements do. They are marketed to athletes as a "fat burner"—a substance that will enhance the utilization of fat during exercise. Fat burners are supposed to increase the use of body fat, spare carbohydrates, and allow athletes to exercise for a longer time before exhaustion. Carnitine is a molecule made from the amino acids lysine and methionine. It is needed to transport fatty acids into the mitochondria, where they are used to produce ATP. Carnitine is not an essential nutrient, and does not need to be supplied in the diet to ensure the efficient use of fatty acids. Supplements are not needed to maintain enough carnitine in the muscle during exercise. Supplements have not been found to increase fat loss, the use of fat as fuel during exercise, or endurance.

WHAT ABOUT MEDIUM CHAIN TRIGLYCERIDES?

Higher levels of fatty acids in the blood increase the availability of fat as a fuel during exercise. If more fat is available, less glucose is used and glycogen is spared so exercise can continue longer. This is the idea behind supplements of **medium chain triglycerides (MCTs)**. These triglycerides provide fatty acids with only 8 to 10 carbons in their molecular structure. They dissolve in water, so they can be absorbed directly into the blood, where muscle cells can use them. Typical dietary triglycerides are made primarily of long-chain fatty acids, which do not dissolve in water. These reach the blood more slowly because they first must be absorbed into the lymphatic system. Medium-chain fatty acids also cross cell membranes easily, and can enter the mitochondria for oxidation without the help of carnitine. Medium-chain triglycerides are marketed to athletes to burn fat, provide an energy source, spare glycogen, and help build muscle. But research has not shown that MCT supplementation does any of these things.

RIBOSE FOR ENERGY?

Ribose is a sugar that is needed to synthesize RNA (ribonucleic acid) and ATP. Marketers of ribose supplements claim that they increase the synthesis of ATP, improve stamina, speed recovery from exercise, and quickly restore ATP levels in the heart and skeletal muscles. Although ribose supplements have been shown to increase ATP production in patients with heart conditions, supplements of ribose have not been found to have any ergogenic effect in healthy people.

CAN HMB PROTECT MUSCLES?

Exercise is good for health, but it does cause some muscle damage. Marketers of **beta-hydroxy-beta-methylbutyrate (HMB)** supplements claim that HMB prevents or slows the muscle damage associated with exercise. HMB is generated from the breakdown of the amino acid leucine. It is found in some foods and is made in the body. HMB appears to be safe, and is a popular supplement among bodybuilders and strength athletes. They use it to promote muscle growth and enhance exercise. Some research supports the effectiveness of HMB for reducing muscle damage and increasing lean body mass, strength, and endurance in trained athletes. But not all studies have found that HMB supplementation has these benefits.

WILL GINSENG KEEP PEOPLE GOING?

Ginseng is an herbal supplement that has been used in Chinese medicine for more than 2,000 years. It is believed to increase resistance to stress, enhance vitality, and increase the physical and mental capacity for work. It is promoted to athletes to increase energy and endurance. However, not all studies have shown that it does so. At recommended doses, ginseng supplements have few reported side effects. Yet, at higher doses, or over longer periods of time, some people report nervousness, agitation, insomnia, diarrhea, headaches, high blood pressure, and heart palpitations. Also, ginseng may increase the effects and side effects of other stimulants, such as caffeine.

EPHEDRA: BANNED BY THE FDA

Ephedrine is the active ingredient in **ephedra**, which comes from the Chinese herb Ma huang. Ephedrine is a stimulant that mimics the effects of epinephrine, a hormone that is released to prepare

AN EPHEDRA DEATH?

The risks of ephedra were dramatically demonstrated in February 2003, when 23-year-old baseball pitcher Steve Bechler died of heat stroke. He had been taking an ephedra-containing supplement to lose weight. Bechler collapsed during a training session in hot, humid Florida weather, and died the next day, when his body temperature reached 108°F (42°C). An autopsy revealed ephedra in his blood, along with smaller amounts of the stimulants pseudoephedrine and caffeine. Did ephedra cause Bechler's death? No one can be sure that he would still be alive if he hadn't taken it. Bechler was slightly overweight and not acclimated to the weather. He was on a weight-loss diet and did not eat the night before he collapsed.

FIGURE 6.4 Steve Bechler, a potential pitcher for the Baltimore Orioles, died suddenly of heatstroke during a training camp in 2003.

Bechler also had high blood pressure and abnormal liver function tests. These were all factors in his death, but ephedra constricts blood vessels causing a rise in body temperature by up to 2°F (17°C), so it may have played a role.

This would not be the first case of a serious problem associated with ephedra. A review of 16,000 reports of adverse effects revealed two deaths, four heart attacks, nine strokes, one seizure, and five psychiatric cases involving ephedra. Even before the FDA ordered ephedra-containing supplements off the shelves, ephedra had been banned by minor league baseball, the National Football League, the National Collegiate Athletic Association, and the International Olympic Committee.

the body for "fight or flight." Like epinephrine, ephedrine increases blood pressure and heart rate. For years, supplements containing ephedrine were marketed to increase body-fat loss, improve athletic performance, and sharpen concentration. The use of ephedrine has been shown to promote weight loss (compared to placebo). But there is little evidence that it enhances physical performance. In fact, ephedrine has serious side effects, including nervousness, headaches, nausea, hypertension, cardiac arrhythmias, heart attack, stroke, and even death. Because of health risks, in 2004 the FDA banned the sale of ephedra-containing supplements. In response to the FDA's ban, the supplement industry formulated "ephedrine-free" products, in which the ephedra is replaced with other herbal stimulants, such as bitter orange. Be aware that these products may have the same side effects as ephedra does.

ANABOLIC STEROIDS: ILLEGAL BULK

Is it worth risking health for bigger muscles? Unfortunately, some athletes think so. They are willing to sacrifice health for the benefits of **anabolic steroids**. The term *anabolic steroid* refers to steroid hormones that speed up protein synthesis and growth. The anabolic steroids used by athletes are synthetic versions of testosterone. Natural testosterone stimulates and maintains the male sexual organs. It also promotes the development of bones and muscles, and the growth of skin and hair. Because of how it is distributed throughout the body, synthetic testosterone used by athletes has a greater effect on muscle development and bone, skin, and hair than it does on sexual organs. When synthetic testosterone is taken in conjunction with exercise and an adequate diet, muscle mass does increase. However, because it increases the amount of testosterone in the body, production of natural testosterone is reduced (Figure 8.3). Without natural testosterone, testicles shrink and sperm production drops off. In adolescents, the use of synthetic testosterone stops bone growth, which stunts height. Anabolic steroid use may also cause oily skin and acne, water retention, yellow eyes and skin, coronary artery disease,

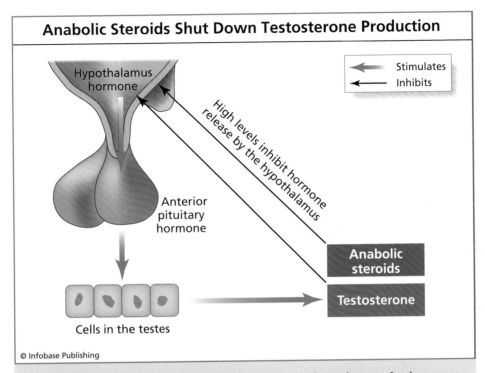

Anabolic Steroids Shut Down Testosterone Production

Hypothalamus hormone

Stimulates
Inhibits

High levels inhibit hormone release by the hypothalamus

Anterior pituitary hormone

Anabolic steroids

Testosterone

Cells in the testes

© Infobase Publishing

FIGURE 8.3 Low testosterone levels activate the release of a hormone that turns on testosterone production by the testes. When there are high levels or either natural or synthetic testosterone, production of this hormone is shut down, so the testes do not make testosterone. Taking anabolic steroids causes the testes to stop producing testosterone.

liver disease, and sometimes death. There also can be psychological and behavioral side effects, such as violent outbursts and depression. Anabolic steroids are illegal, so their manufacture and distribution is not regulated. Users can never be sure of the potency or purity of what they are taking.

ARE STEROID PRECURSORS SAFER THAN ANABOLIC STEROIDS?

Steroid precursors may sound like the perfect alternative to anabolic steroids. These are compounds that can be converted into steroid hormones in the body. They include androstenedione, androstenediol, DHEA, norandrostenediol, and norandrostenedione. They have been marketed as alternatives to anabolic steroids to increase muscle mass. Yet, many people wonder if they work and if they are safe.

The best known of the steroid precursors is androstenedione, often referred to as "andro." It is a precursor to testosterone and is marketed to increase levels of testosterone. Bodybuilders have used andro for years, but it was launched to public prominence when major league baseball player Mark McGwire announced that he used it during the 1998 season. That year, he hit 70 home runs, breaking the league's single-season record. McGwire has subsequently stopped using andro.

Did andro help McGwire hit all those home runs? Probably not. Studies have not shown that it helps athletes. But it has been shown to increase the risk of heart disease. Because steroid precursors are converted into estrogen and testosterone in the body, they may cause hormonal imbalances. In men, these imbalances can lead to testicular shrinkage and breast enlargement. In women, they can lead to baldness, a deepening voice, increased growth of facial hair, and abnormal menstrual cycles. The risks are greatest in children and adolescents, where andro may cause early puberty and stunted bone growth.

As with anabolic steroids, steroid precursors are now classified as controlled substances and cannot be sold as dietary supplements. Andro is banned by all major national and international sports organizations.

PEPTIDE HORMONES ARE BY PRESCRIPTION ONLY

Peptide hormones are hormones made from chains of amino acids. Peptide hormones can be made in a laboratory. They are illegal unless prescribed by a physician. Most have dangerous side effects. It is difficult to detect these drugs in athletes because they are present naturally, broken down rapidly, and excreted in urine only in small amounts.

Does Growth Hormone Grow Muscles?

Human **growth hormone** is a peptide hormone that is produced by the pituitary gland. It is important for bone and muscle growth during childhood. Genetically engineered growth hormone is used to treat children who are small due to growth hormone deficiency. In adults, growth hormone maintains lean tissue, stimulates fat breakdown, increases the number of red blood cells, and boosts heart function. This hormone is appealing to athletes because it increases muscle protein synthesis. However, the ergogenic benefits of growth hormone among athletes remain unproven. More important, prolonged use of growth hormone can cause heart disease and high blood pressure, bone and joint pain, and excessive bone growth that enlarges the hands and feet and alters facial features. Growth hormone is on the World Anti-Doping Agency's list of banned substances.

Erythropoietin (EPO): The Blood Booster

Another peptide hormone that is popular among endurance athletes is **erythropoietin,** known as EPO. The kidneys make erythropoietin. It stimulates the production of red blood cells in the bone marrow. Genetically engineered EPO is given to patients with kidney disease, who cannot produce enough erythropoietin. It also is given to people who have anemia due to chemotherapy, HIV infection, or blood loss. EPO can enhance the performance of endurance athletes because it increases the number of red blood cells, which increases the body's ability to transport oxygen to the muscles. It therefore increases the ability to use aerobic metabolism and spares glycogen. However, too much EPO can lead to too many red blood cells. This can cause excessive blood clotting, heart attacks, and strokes. The International Olympic Committee banned EPO in 1990 after it was linked to the death of more than a dozen cyclists.

OTHER SUPPLEMENTS

The list of things athletes will ingest to enhance performance is endless. It includes such substances as bee pollen, brewer's yeast, wheat germ oil, royal jelly, and DNA and RNA.

Bee pollen is a mixture of the pollen of flowering plants, plant nectar, and bee saliva. It contains no extraordinary factors and has not been shown to have any performance-enhancing effects. In addition, ingesting or inhaling bee pollen can be hazardous to people who are allergic to various plant pollens.

Brewer's yeast is a source of B vitamins and some minerals, but has not been demonstrated to have any ergogenic properties. Likewise, there is no evidence to support claims that wheat germ oil will aid endurance. As an oil, it is high in fat, but it is not a better energy source than any other fat.

Royal jelly is a substance produced by worker bees to feed the queen bee. Although it helps the queen bee to grow twice the size of worker bees and to live 40 times longer, royal jelly does not appear to enhance athletic capacity in humans.

Finally, DNA and RNA are marketed to aid in tissue regeneration. In the body, they carry genetic information and are needed to synthesize proteins, but DNA and RNA are not required in the diet, and supplements do not help replace damaged cells.

REVIEW

Anything designed to enhance performance can be considered an ergogenic aid. Many of these products provide more of a psychological advantage than a physiological edge. Dietary supplements marketed as ergogenic aids include vitamins, minerals, proteins, amino acids, lipids, herbs, hormones, and substances made by the body. Some, such as antioxidant supplements, are relatively harmless but have not been shown to enhance performance. Others, such as creatine, bicarbonate, HMB, and caffeine are not associated with serious side effects and may enhance performance in certain types of activities. Some others, such as anabolic steroids and EPO, can enhance performance but are dangerous to health. Many ergogenic supplements are illegal in both amateur and professional athletics. When considering the use of an ergogenic supplement, it is important to weigh the health risks against potential benefits. Just because a product is sold doesn't make it safe, and just because something appears in print does not make it true. Choosing to use an ergogenic aid should be a serious decision that is discussed with a doctor. Many of these supplements have dangerous interactions with other drugs. They also can make existing health conditions worse.

9

NUTRITIONAL PROBLEMS COMMON AMONG ATHLETES

Sometimes, in an effort to improve performance or achieve unrealistic goals, athletes may consume unhealthy diets or push their bodies too hard. The consequences may actually end up hurting performance and overall health.

LOSING AND GAINING WEIGHT

How much an athlete weighs can affect their speed, endurance, and power, while the amounts of muscle and fat a person has will influence strength, agility, and appearance. Athletes often try to lose or gain weight to optimize performance. Those involved in activities in which small, lean bodies offer an advantage—such as gymnastics and certain running events—may restrict food intake to maintain a low body weight. Athletes involved in sports such as football or rugby may try to gain weight and strength to give them a competitive advantage. Those involved in sports with

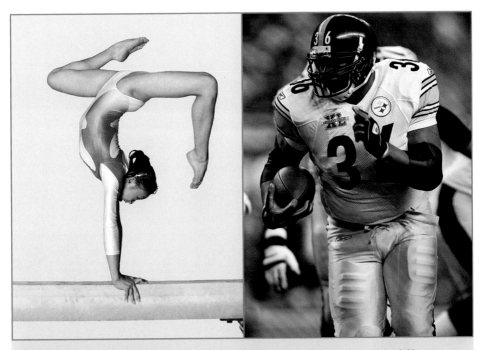

FIGURE 9.1 Different body compositions are appropriate for different sports. Although both gymnasts and football players have significant muscle mass, gymnasts are usually thin and lean, while football players are generally more bulky. These very different body types are advantageous in different sports.

weight classes may aim for a specific weight to be at the high end of a lower weight class (Figure 9.1).

Athletes' concerns about body weight and their proportions of muscle and body fat may lead to unhealthy weight-loss practices or eating disorders. Regardless of their sport, athletes should aim for a healthy weight. This is a weight that can realistically be maintained, allows for improvement in exercise performance, minimizes the chance of injury or illness, and reduces the risk of chronic disease. Weight changes, whether to increase or decrease body weight, should be accomplished slowly in the off-season or at the beginning of the season, before competition begins.

How to Gain Weight Safely

To gain weight, a person must increase energy intake by 500 to 1,000 calories per day. This can be accomplished by snacking on high-calorie foods and beverages, such as cheese, peanut butter, fruit juices, and ice cream. Muscle-building exercises should be increased to ensure that lean tissue is gained, rather than fat. The rate that weight is gained will depend on the person's genetic makeup, how many extra calories are consumed, and the type of training program that is followed.

"MAKING WEIGHT" CAN BE DANGEROUS

"Making weight" refers to the practice of altering body weight to fit into a set weight category. For example, sports with weight classes, such as wrestling, may require an athlete to gain or lose weight to fit into a particular class. Competing at the high end of a weight class is believed to give the athlete an advantage over smaller opponents. But weight changes are not necessarily beneficial to an athlete's health or performance. One strategy for cutting weight is to dehydrate. This is accomplished through practices such as vigorous exercise, fluid restriction, exercising while wearing rubber sweat suits, and sitting in hot environments, such as saunas and steam rooms. More extreme, rapid weight-loss measures include intentional vomiting and the use of diuretics and laxatives. All of these practices interfere with water and electrolyte balance. They can impair performance and adversely affect heart function, kidney function, and temperature regulation. They can even be fatal. In 1997, three young wrestlers died while exercising in rubber suits in order to sweat off water. As a result, wrestling weight classes were altered to eliminate the lightest class, rubber and other impermeable sweat suits were banned, a maximum wrestling room temperature of 75°F (24°C) was established, weigh-ins were moved to one hour before competition, and mandatory weight-loss rules were instituted. College wrestlers cannot have less than 5% body fat; high school wrestlers cannot have less than 7%.

How to Lose Weight Safely

To lose weight and remain healthy, a person must reduce energy intake enough to allow gradual weight loss while maintaining a healthy diet. Decreasing normal calorie intake by 10% will allow weight loss without feelings of hunger or deprivation. For example, if an athlete's normal intake is 3,000 calories per day, decreasing this by 300 calories (the amount in a cup of ice cream) should cause a slow weight loss. To preserve muscle and other lean tissue and enhance fat loss, weight loss should take place at a rate of 1/2 to 2 pounds (0.2 to 1 kg) per week, and activity levels should be maintained or increased. Dieting to maintain an unrealistically low weight may threaten nutritional status, health, and athletic performance.

EATING DISORDERS: ATHLETES AT RISK

Eating disorders are a group of conditions that are characterized by a pathological concern with body weight and shape. They are primarily psychological disorders, but they involve nutrition-related behaviors and complications. Athletes are under extreme pressure to achieve and maintain a body weight that optimizes performance. Failure to meet weight-loss goals may have serious consequences, such as being cut from a team or restricted from competition. This pressure may cause some athletes to follow strict diets and maintain body weights that are not healthy. This, combined with the self-motivation and discipline that characterizes successful athletes, makes many athletes vulnerable to eating disorders. Eating disorders are more common in female athletes than in male ones. They are more common in sports where leanness or low body weight are expected or are an advantage, such as ballet, gymnastics, track and field, cycling, crew, wrestling, and horse racing.

Athletes with Anorexia

One type of eating disorder that may occur among athletes is **anorexia nervosa**. Anorexia nervosa is characterized by the loss of 15% or more of body weight. Weight is lost by restricting food intake and using behaviors such as vomiting after eating, abuse of laxatives, and excessive exercise to eliminate or use up calories. People with anorexia are generally very secretive about their eating behaviors. An athlete's regimented schedule makes it easy for him or her to use training diets and timetables, travel, or competition as an excuse not to eat normally. Over time, continued starvation leads to serious health problems, as well as a decline in athletic performance. Starvation can lead to abnormal heart rhythms, low blood pressure, and atrophy of the heart muscle. The lack of energy and nutrients means that activity and growth are not supported. Sleep disorders are also common in people with anorexia.

Binging and Purging: Bulimia

Among athletes, the eating disorder **bulimia nervosa** is more common than anorexia. It is characterized by a cycle of binging and purging. Binging is the rapid consumption of a large amount of food in a short amount of time. This is accompanied by feelings of guilt and shame. Purging refers to methods used to eliminate excess calories from the body. These include self-induced vomiting, misuse of laxatives and diuretics, and excessive dieting and exercise. Bulimia may begin when an athlete is unable to stick to a restrictive diet, or because the hunger associated with a very low-calorie diet leads to an episode of overeating. Those with bulimia are usually of normal or slightly higher than normal body weight. Most of the health complications associated with bulimia—including tooth decay from repeated vomiting and dangerous changes in body chemistry—are a result of the binge-purge cycle.

Compulsive Exercising

The use of compulsive exercise to control weight has been termed anorexia athletica. It has less to do with food than either anorexia or bulimia, but it is nonetheless considered an eating disorder. People with this disorder use extreme training as a way to purge calories. This behavior is easy to justify because it is a common belief that serious athletes can never work too hard or too long. Compulsive exercisers will force themselves to exercise even when they don't feel well and may miss social events in order to fulfill

THE RISK OF EATING DISORDERS IS GREATER IN SOME SPORTS

Ninety-three percent of eating disorders among athletes involve women's sports. The most problematic are women's cross country, women's gymnastics, women's swimming, and women's track and field events. The male sports with the highest number of participants with eating disorders are wrestling and cross country.

their exercise quota. They often calculate exercise goals based on how much they eat. They believe that any break in training will cause them to gain weight and their performance to suffer. Compulsive exercise can lead to more serious eating disorders, such as anorexia and bulimia. It also may bring on severe health problems, including kidney failure, heart attack, and death.

THE FEMALE ATHLETE TRIAD

In female athletes, the desire to reduce body weight and fat to improve performance, achieve what is perceived as an ideal body, and meet goals (often goals set by coaches, trainers, or parents) increases the risk for a syndrome of interrelated disorders referred to as the **female athlete triad.** This involves a complex set of relationships among energy, menstrual status, and bone health.

As discussed above, many athletes try to maintain a low body weight. A combination of low energy intake and high energy output can alter the secretion of reproductive hormones. This may lead to **amenorrhea**, the absence of menstruation. Amenorrhea is accompanied by low levels of estrogen, a hormone that is important for bone health. Low estrogen decreases calcium absorption from the diet and affects calcium balance at the bone. This results in reduced bone density. Female athletes also tend to not eat enough calcium-containing foods. The combination of low estrogen levels and poor calcium intake leads to premature bone loss, failure to reach a

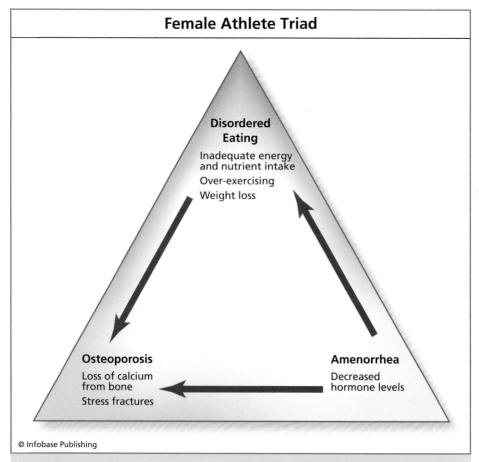

Female Athlete Triad

Disordered Eating

Inadequate energy and nutrient intake

Over-exercising

Weight loss

Osteoporosis

Loss of calcium from bone

Stress fractures

Amenorrhea

Decreased hormone levels

© Infobase Publishing

FIGURE 9.2 Female athletes training to be lighter, stronger, and faster face unique problems in maintaining a high level of performance and good health. The female athlete triad is a dangerous combination of interrelated disorders that can occur in female athletes who restrict their caloric intake.

healthy bone mass, and an increased risk of osteoporosis (Figure 9.2). The most significant short-term health consequence of the female athlete triad is an increase in the incidence of stress fractures.

Exercise, particularly weight-bearing exercise, generally increases bone density. This reduces the risk of osteoporosis. However, when estrogen levels are low due to amenorrhea, neither enough dietary calcium nor the increase in bone mass brought about by weight-bearing exercise can make up for the bone loss. If the menstrual cycle resumes, bone loss can at least be partially reversed, but it is not known whether these athletes are at greater risk for osteoporosis later in life.

MORE ISN'T ALWAYS BETTER: OVERTRAINING SYNDROME

Most athletes believe that training harder improves their performance, but this isn't always the case. It turns out that enough rest is just as important as enough training. Muscle strength and cardiovascular and respiratory fitness improve in response to the stress of exercise training. Initially, training can cause fatigue and weakness, but during rest periods, the body rebuilds to become stronger. If not enough rest occurs between exercise sessions, there is no time for the body to rebuild. Fitness and performance do not improve. In competitive athletes, excessive training without enough rest can lead to **overtraining syndrome**. This involves emotional, behavioral, and physical symptoms that last for weeks to months. The most common symptom is fatigue that not only limits workouts, but also is felt even at rest. Some athletes experience a decrease in appetite and weight loss as well as muscle soreness, increased frequency of colds and other viral illnesses, and higher incidence

SWIMMING HALF THE TIME

It is often thought that more training is better when it comes to improving performance, but a study involving a group of swimmers has shown otherwise. Half of the swimmers trained for 90 minutes in the morning and another 90 minutes in the afternoon. The other half trained only for 90 minutes in the afternoon. The first group of swimmers had a decline in speed over time, while the other group improved their speed. Doubling the training did not enhance performance.

of injuries. They may become moody, easily irritated, or depressed. They may have altered sleep patterns or lose their competitive desire and enthusiasm. Although overtraining syndrome occurs only in serious athletes who are working out extensively, rest is essential for anyone who is trying to improve fitness.

LOW IRON MEANS POOR PERFORMANCE

Low iron stores are one of the most common nutritional problems seen in athletes. The condition is particularly common in female athletes. If it progresses to iron deficiency anemia, it can impair athletic performance as well as reduce immune function and affect other physiological processes.

Low iron stores may be caused by:

- Not enough iron in the diet
- A rise in the body's demand for iron
- Increased iron losses
- A redistribution of iron due to exercise

Female athletes' iron needs are higher than those of male athletes because they need to replace the iron lost in menstrual blood. In athletes of both sexes, inadequate iron intake often contributes to low iron stores. Dietary iron intake may be low in athletes who restrict food intake to keep body weight low, or in those who consume a vegetarian diet; red meat is an excellent source of an easily absorbed form of iron. If iron deficiency progresses to anemia, the body's ability to transport oxygen and produce ATP by aerobic metabolism is reduced.

Iron needs may be increased in athletes because exercise stimulates the production of red blood cells, so more iron is needed for hemoglobin synthesis. Iron also is needed for the synthesis of muscle myoglobin and the iron-containing proteins needed for ATP production in the mitochondria. Prolonged training also may increase iron losses, possibly because of increased fecal, urinary, and sweat losses. Iron balance may also be affected by the breaking of red blood cells from impact in events such as running. This rarely causes anemia, because the breaking of red blood cells stimulates the production of new ones. Although a specific RDA has not been set for athletes, the DRIs acknowledge that the requirement for iron may be 30% to 70% higher for athletes than for the general population.

Some athletes experience a condition known as sports anemia, which is a temporary decrease in hemoglobin concentration during exercise training. It occurs when the blood volume increases to improve oxygen delivery, but the synthesis of red blood cells lags behind. This reduces the number of red blood cells per milliliter of blood. This phenomenon is an adaptation to training and does not seem to affect the delivery of oxygen to tissues.

VEGETARIAN DIETS FOR ATHLETES

Vegetarian diets exclude or partially exclude animal products. These diets are generally healthy, but in athletes they may increase the risk of certain nutritional problems. Athletes often have very high caloric requirements. Although in most cases it is easy to meet energy needs by eating a vegetarian diet, the number of calories may be low if the diet is very high in fiber. The best way to determine if energy needs are being met by the diet is to monitor body weight and composition.

Vegetarian diets tend to be lower in protein than omnivorous diets. The quality of the protein in vegetarian diets is adequate, but plant proteins are not digested as easily as animal proteins. To compensate for this, protein intake should be increased by about 10%; vegetarian athletes should consume 1.3 to 1.8 grams of protein per kilogram of body weight. That is the equivalent of 90 to 130 grams of protein for a 154-pound (70-kg) person. Athletes with relatively low energy requirements need to choose foods carefully to ensure that their protein intakes meet these recommendations.

Vegetarian athletes may be at risk for low intake of a number of vitamins and minerals, including vitamin B_{12}, vitamin D, riboflavin, iron, calcium, and zinc. The best dietary sources of these nutrients are animal products. Milk is a good source of calcium, vitamin D, vitamin B_{12}, and riboflavin, so vegetarians who consume dairy products are less likely than vegans (vegetarians who consume no animal products) to have low intakes of these. As discussed above, iron is of particular concern to the athlete. The iron in plant foods is not absorbed as efficiently as the iron found in animal foods. Vegetarians tend to have lower iron stores than nonvegetarians, even when iron intake is the same. Given that exercise may increase iron needs, vegetarian athletes, especially women, are at greater risk of low iron status.

Some athletes, especially women, may switch to a vegetarian diet as a means to lose weight and attain a leaner body. In some cases, this can indicate that an athlete is at risk for developing an eating disorder.

REVIEW

In an effort to improve performance, athletes may engage in certain practices, such as restricting food intake or training excessively, that increase the possibility of injury or illness. Health problems often occur as a result of attempts to lose or gain body weight. Severe weight-loss diets and the use of dehydration to achieve short-term weight loss can impair health and performance. Some athletes who are concerned about their weight may develop eating disorders. When these occur in women, they may lead to amenorrhea and osteoporosis. The combination of these three conditions is referred to as the female athlete triad. It has long-term consequences for bone health. Excessive training can lead to overtraining syndrome, which is characterized by fatigue, more frequent colds and other viral illnesses, and increased risk for injuries. Iron deficiency also is a common problem in athletes, particularly females. Poor iron status may be caused by an inadequate iron intake, an increased demand for iron, increased iron losses, or a redistribution of iron due to exercise training. Some athletes may be at risk for deficiencies of iron, calcium, vitamin B_{12}, vitamin D, riboflavin, and zinc because they eat vegetarian diets. In order to maintain health while remaining physically active, it is important to follow a diet that meets nutrient needs and to keep training at a reasonable level.

APPENDIX A

DIETARY REFERENCE INTAKES

ACCEPTABLE MACRONUTRIENT DISTRIBUTION RANGES (AMDR) FOR HEALTHY DIETS AS A PERCENTAGE OF ENERGY

Age	Carbohydrates	Added Sugars	Total Fat	Linoleic Acid	α-Linolenic Acid	Protein
1–3 years old	45–65	25	30–40	5–10	0.6–1.2	5–20
4–18 years old	45–65	25	25–35	5–10	0.6–1.2	10–30
≥ 19 years old	45–65	25	20–35	5–10	0.6–1.2	10–35

Source: Institute of Medicine, Food and Nutrition Board. "Dietary Reference Intakes for Energy, Carbohydrates, Fiber, Fat, Protein, and Amino Acids." Washington, D.C.: National Academies Press, 2002.

RECOMMENDED INTAKES OF VITAMINS FOR VARIOUS AGE GROUPS

Life Stage	Vit A (µg/day)	Vit C (mg/day)	Vit D (µg/day)	Vit E (mg/day)	Vit K (µg/day)
Infants					
0–6 mo	400	40	5	4	2.0
7–12 mo	500	50	5	5	2.5
Children					
1–3 yrs	**300**	**15**	5	**6**	30
4–8 yrs	**400**	**25**	5	**7**	55
Males					
9–13 yrs	**600**	**45**	5	**11**	60
14–18 yrs	**900**	**75**	5	**15**	75
19–30 yrs	**900**	**90**	5	**15**	120
31–50 yrs	**900**	**90**	5	**15**	120
51–70 yrs	**900**	**90**	10	**15**	120
>70 yrs	**900**	**90**	15	**15**	120
Females					
9–13 yrs	**600**	**45**	5	**11**	60
14–18 yrs	**700**	**65**	5	**15**	75
19–30 yrs	**700**	**75**	5	**15**	90
31–50 yrs	**700**	**75**	5	**15**	90
51–70 yrs	**700**	**75**	10	**15**	90
>70 yrs	**700**	**75**	15	**15**	90
Pregnancy					
≤18 yrs	**750**	**80**	5	**15**	75
19–30 yrs	**770**	**85**	5	**15**	90
31–50 yrs	**770**	**85**	5	**15**	90
Lactation					
≤18 yrs	**1,200**	**115**	5	**19**	75
19–30 yrs	**1,300**	**120**	5	**19**	90
31–50 yrs	**1,300**	**120**	5	**19**	90

RECOMMENDED INTAKES OF VITAMINS
FOR VARIOUS AGE GROUPS (continued)

Life Stage	Thiamin (mg/day)	Riboflavin (mg/day)	Niacin (mg/day)	Vit B$_6$ (mg/day)	Folate (µg/day)
Infants					
0–6 mo	0.2	0.3	2	0.1	65
7–12 mo	0.3	0.4	4	0.3	80
Children					
1–3 yrs	0.5	0.5	6	0.5	150
4–8 yrs	0.6	0.6	8	0.6	200
Males					
9–13 yrs	0.9	0.9	12	1.0	300
14–18 yrs	1.2	1.3	16	1.3	400
19–30 yrs	1.2	1.3	16	1.3	400
31–50 yrs	1.2	1.3	16	1.3	400
51–70 yrs	1.2	1.3	16	1.7	400
>70 yrs	1.2	1.3	16	1.7	400
Females					
9–13 yrs	0.9	0.9	12	1.0	300
14–18 yrs	1.0	1.0	14	1.2	400
19–30 yrs	1.1	1.1	14	1.3	400
31–50 yrs	1.1	1.1	14	1.3	400
51–70 yrs	1.1	1.1	14	1.5	400
>70 yrs	1.1	1.1	14	1.5	400
Pregnancy					
≤18 yrs	1.4	1.4	18	1.9	600
19–30 yrs	1.4	1.4	18	1.9	600
31–50 yrs	1.4	1.4	18	1.9	600
Lactation					
≤18 yrs	1.4	1.6	17	2.0	500
19–30 yrs	1.4	1.6	17	2.0	500
31–50 yrs	1.4	1.6	17	2.0	500

(continues)

RECOMMENDED INTAKES OF VITAMINS FOR VARIOUS AGE GROUPS (continued)

Life Stage	Vit B$_{12}$ (µg/day)	Pantothenic Acid (mg/day)	Biotin Group (µg/day)	Choline* (mg/day)
Infants				
0–6 mo	0.4	1.7	5	125
7–12 mo	0.5	1.8	6	150
Children				
1–3 yrs	0.9	2	8	200
4–8 yrs	1.2	3	12	250
Males				
9–13 yrs	1.8	4	20	375
14–18 yrs	2.4	5	25	550
19–30 yrs	2.4	5	30	550
31–50 yrs	2.4	5	30	550
51–70 yrs	2.4	5	30	550
>70 yrs	2.4	5	30	550
Females				
9–13 yrs	1.8	4	20	375
14–18 yrs	2.4	5	25	400
19–30 yrs	2.4	5	30	425
31–50 yrs	2.4	5	30	425
51–70 yrs	2.4	5	30	425
>70 yrs	2.4	5	30	425
Pregnancy				
≤18 yrs	2.6	6	30	450
19–30 yrs	2.6	6	30	450
31–50 yrs	2.6	6	30	450
Lactation				
≤18 yrs	2.8	7	35	550
19–30 yrs	2.8	7	35	550
31–50 yrs	2.8	7	35	550

Note: This table presents Recommended Dietary Allowances (RDAs) in bold type and Adequate Intakes (AIs) in ordinary type.

* Not yet classified as a vitamin

Source: Adapted from Dietary Reference Intake Tables: The Complete Set. *Institute of Medicine, National Academy of Sciences. Available online at www.nap.edu.*

RECOMMENDED INTAKES OF SELECTED MINERALS FOR VARIOUS AGE GROUPS

Life Stage	Calcium (mg/day)	Chromium (µg/day)	Copper (µg/day)	Fluroide (mg/day)	Iodine (µg/day)
Infants					
0–6 mo	210	0.2	200	0.01	110
7–12 mo	270	5.5	220	0.5	130
Children					
1–3 yrs	500	11	**340**	0.7	**90**
4–8 yrs	800	15	**440**	1	**90**
Males					
9–13 yrs	1,300	25	**700**	2	**120**
14–18 yrs	1,300	35	**890**	3	**150**
19–30 yrs	1,000	35	**900**	4	**150**
31–50 yrs	1,000	35	**900**	4	**150**
51–70 yrs	1,200	30	**900**	4	**150**
>70 yrs	1,200	30	**900**	4	**150**
Females					
9–13 yrs	1,300	21	**700**	2	**120**
14–18 yrs	1,300	24	**890**	3	**150**
19–30 yrs	1,000	25	**900**	3	**150**
31–50 yrs	1,000	25	**900**	3	**150**
51–70 yrs	1,200	20	**900**	3	**150**
>70 yrs	1,200	20	**900**	3	**150**
Pregnancy					
≤18 yrs	1,300	29	**1,000**	3	**220**
19–30 yrs	1,000	30	**1,000**	3	**220**
31–50 yrs	1,000	30	**1,000**	3	**220**
Lactation					
≤18 yrs	1,300	44	**1,300**	3	**290**
19–30 yrs	1,000	45	**1,300**	3	**290**
31–50 yrs	1,000	45	**1,300**	3	**290**

(continues)

RECOMMENDED INTAKES OF SELECTED MINERALS FOR VARIOUS AGE GROUPS (continued)

Life Stage	Iron (mg/day)	Magnesium (mg/day)	Phosphorus (mg/day)	Selenium (µg/day)
Infants				
0–6 mo	0.27	30	100	15
7–12 mo	11	75	275	20
Children				
1–3 yrs	7	80	460	20
4–8 yrs	10	130	500	30
Males				
9–13 yrs	8	240	1,250	40
14–18 yrs	11	410	1,250	55
19–30 yrs	8	400	700	55
31–50 yrs	8	420	700	55
51–70 yrs	8	420	700	55
>70 yrs	8	420	700	55
Females				
9–13 yrs	8	240	1,250	40
14–18 yrs	15	360	1,250	55
19–30 yrs	18	310	700	55
31–50 yrs	18	320	700	55
51–70 yrs	8	320	700	55
>70 yrs	8	320	700	55
Pregnancy				
≤18 yrs	27	400	1,250	60
19–30 yrs	27	350	700	60
31–50 yrs	27	360	700	60
Lactation				
≤18 yrs	10	360	1,250	70
19–30 yrs	9	310	700	70
31–50 yrs	9	320	700	70

RECOMMENDED INTAKES OF SELECTED MINERALS FOR VARIOUS AGE GROUPS (continued)

Life Stage	Zinc (mg/day)	Sodium (g/day)	Chloride (g/day)	Potassium (g/day)
Infants				
0–6 mo	2	0.12	0.18	0.4
7–12 mo	**3**	0.37	0.57	0.7
Children				
1–3 yrs	**3**	1.0	1.5	3.0
4–8 yrs	**5**	1.2	1.9	3.8
Males				
9–13 yrs	**8**	1.5	2.3	4.5
14–18 yrs	**11**	1.5	2.3	4.7
19–30 yrs	**11**	1.5	2.3	4.7
31–50 yrs	**11**	1.5	2.3	4.7
51–70 yrs	**11**	1.3	2.0	4.7
>70 yrs	**11**	1.2	1.8	4.7
Females				
9–13 yrs	**8**	1.5	2.3	4.5
14–18 yrs	**9**	1.5	2.3	4.7
19–30 yrs	**8**	1.5	2.3	4.7
31–50 yrs	**8**	1.5	2.3	4.7
51–70 yrs	**8**	1.3	2.0	4.7
>70 yrs	**8**	1.2	1.8	4.7
Pregnancy				
≤18 yrs	**13**	1.5	2.3	4.7
19–30 yrs	**11**	1.5	2.3	4.7
31–50 yrs	**11**	1.5	2.3	4.7
Lactation				
≤18 yrs	**14**	1.5	2.3	5.1
19–30 yrs	**12**	1.5	2.3	5.1
31–50 yrs	**12**	1.5	2.3	5.1

Note: This table presents Recommended Dietary Allowances (RDAs) in bold type and Adequate Intakes (AIs) in ordinary type.

Source: Adapted from Dietary Reference Intake Tables: The Complete Set. Institute of Medicine, National Academy of Sciences. Available online at www.nap.edu.

APPENDIX B

HEALTHY BODY WEIGHTS
Body Mass Index (BMI)

Body mass index, or BMI, is the measurement of choice for determining health risks associated with body weight. BMI uses a mathematical formula that takes into account both a person's height and weight. BMI equals a person's weight in kilograms divided by height in meters squared ($BMI = kg/m^2$).

RISK OF ASSOCIATED DISEASE ACCORDING TO BMI AND WAIST SIZE FOR ADULTS			
BMI		**Waist less than or equal to 40 in. (men) or 35 in. (women)**	**Waist greater than 40 in. (men) or 35 in. (women)**
18.5 or less	Underweight	N/A	N/A
18.5–24.9	Normal	N/A	N/A
25.0–29.9	Overweight	Increased	High
30.0–34.9	Obese	High	Very High
35.0–39.9	Obese	Very High	Very High
40 or greater	Extremely Obese	Extremely High	Extremely High

Determining Your Body Mass Index (BMI)

To use the table on the following page, find the appropriate height in the left-hand column. Move across the row to the given weight. The number at the top of the column is the BMI for that height and weight. Then use the table above to determine how at risk you are for developing a weight-related disease.

BMI (kg/m²) Height (in.)	19	20	21	22	23	24	25 Weight (lb)	26	27	28	29	30	35	40
58	91	96	100	105	110	115	119	124	129	134	138	143	167	191
59	94	99	104	109	114	119	124	128	133	138	143	148	173	198
60	97	102	107	112	118	123	128	133	138	143	148	153	179	204
61	100	106	111	116	122	127	132	137	143	148	153	158	185	211
62	104	109	115	120	126	131	136	142	147	153	158	164	191	218
63	107	113	118	124	130	135	141	146	152	158	163	169	197	225
64	110	116	122	128	134	140	145	151	157	163	169	174	204	232
65	114	120	126	132	138	144	150	156	162	168	174	180	210	240
66	118	124	130	136	142	148	155	161	167	173	179	186	216	247
67	121	127	134	140	146	153	159	166	172	178	185	191	223	255
68	125	131	138	144	151	158	164	171	177	184	190	197	230	262
69	128	135	142	149	155	162	169	176	182	189	196	203	236	270
70	132	139	146	153	160	167	174	181	188	195	202	207	243	278
71	136	143	150	157	165	172	179	186	193	200	208	215	250	286
72	140	147	154	162	169	177	184	191	199	206	213	221	258	294
73	144	151	159	166	174	182	189	197	204	212	219	227	265	302
74	148	155	163	171	179	186	194	202	210	218	225	233	272	311
75	152	160	168	176	184	192	200	208	216	224	232	240	279	319
76	156	164	172	180	189	197	205	213	221	230	238	246	287	328

Source: Adapted from Partnership for Healthy Weight Management, http://www.consumer.gov/weightloss/bmi.htm.

BMI-FOR-AGE GROWTH CHARTS

2 to 20 years: Boys
Body mass index-for-age percentiles

NAME _____

RECORD # _____

Date	Age	Weight	Stature	BMI*	Comments

*To Calculate BMI: Weight (kg) ÷ Stature (cm) ÷ Stature (cm) x 10,000
or Weight (lb) ÷ Stature (in) ÷ Stature (in) x 703

BMI
35
34
33
32
31
30
29
28
27
26
25
24
23
22
21
20
19
18
17
16
15
14
13
12

BMI
27
26
25
24
23
22
21
20
19
18
17
16
15
14
13
12

kg/m²

AGE (YEARS)

kg/m²

2 3 4 5 6 7 8 9 10 11 12 13 14 15 16 17 18 19 20

95
90
85
75
50
25
10
5

Published May 30, 2000 (modified 10/16/00).
SOURCE: Developed by the National Center for Health Statistics in collaboration with
the National Center for Chronic Disease Prevention and Health Promotion (2000).
http://www.cdc.gov/growthcharts

SAFER · HEALTHIER · PEOPLE™

2 to 20 years: Girls
Body mass index-for-age percentiles

NAME _____

RECORD # _____

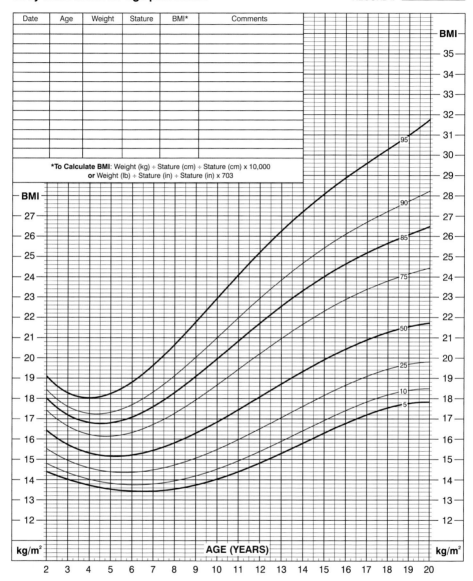

Date	Age	Weight	Stature	BMI*	Comments

*To Calculate BMI: Weight (kg) ÷ Stature (cm) ÷ Stature (cm) x 10,000
or Weight (lb) ÷ Stature (in) ÷ Stature (in) x 703

AGE (YEARS)

Published May 30, 2000 (modified 10/16/00).
SOURCE: Developed by the National Center for Health Statistics in collaboration with
the National Center for Chronic Disease Prevention and Health Promotion (2000).
http://www.cdc.gov/growthcharts

SAFER·HEALTHIER·PEOPLE™

APPENDIX C

BLOOD VALUES OF NUTRITIONAL RELEVANCE

Red blood cells	
Men	4.6–6.2 million/mm^3
Women	4.2–5.2 million/mm^3
White blood cells	5,000–10,000/mm^3
Calcium	9–11 mg/100 mL
Iron	
Men	75–175 µg/100 mL
Women	65–165 µg/100 mL
Zinc	0.75–1.4 µg/mL
Potassium	3.5–5.0 mEq/L
Sodium	136–145 mEq/L
Vitamin A	20–80 µg/100 mL
Vitamin B$_{12}$	200–800 pg/100 mL
Vitamin C	0.6–2.0 mg/100 mL
Folate	2–20 ng/mL
pH	7.35–7.45
Total protein	6.6–8.0 g/100 mL
Albumin	3.0–4.0 g/100 mL
Cholesterol	less than 200 mg/100 mL
Glucose	60–100 mg/100 mL blood, 70–120 mg/100 mL serum

Source: Handbook of Clinical Dietetics, *American Dietetic Association (New Haven, Conn.: Yale University Press, 1981); and Committee on Dietetics of the Mayo Clinic,* Mayo Clinic Diet Manual *(Philadelphia: W. B. Saunders Company, 1981), pp. 275–277.*

APPENDIX D

USDA'S MYPYRAMID

Source http://www.mypyramid.gov/downloads/MyPyramid_Anatomy.pdf.

# GLOSSARY

Acetyl-CoA   An intermediate formed during the breakdown of carbohydrates, fatty acids, and amino acids; it consists of a 2-carbon compound attached to a molecule of coenzyme A (CoA).

Actin   The contractile protein that makes up the thin filaments in muscle fibers

Adequate intakes (AIs)   DRI values are used as a goal for intake when there is not enough evidence to establish a recommended dietary allowance (RDA)

Adipose tissue   Tissue found under the skin and around body organs that is composed of fat-storing cells

Aerobic capacity (also called maximum oxygen consumption and VO$_2$max)   A person's maximum capacity to generate ATP by aerobic metabolism; it depends on the amount of oxygen that can be delivered to and used by the muscle.

Aerobic exercise   Activity that uses aerobic metabolism and improves cardiovascular fitness

Aerobic metabolism   Metabolism requiring oxygen; the complete breakdown of glucose, fatty acids, and amino acids to carbon dioxide and water occurs only via aerobic metabolism.

Aldosterone   A hormone that increases sodium reabsorption and therefore enhances water retention by the kidneys

Amenorrhea   Absence of menstrual periods in women

Amino acids   Nitrogen-containing organic compounds that function as the building blocks of proteins

Anabolic steroids   Synthetic, fat-soluble hormones used by some athletes to increase muscle mass

Anaerobic metabolism   The production of ATP from glucose in the absence of oxygen; also called anaerobic glycolysis.

Angiotensin II   A compound that causes blood vessel walls to constrict and stimulates the release of the hormone aldosterone

Anorexia nervosa   An eating disorder that is characterized by a distorted body image, self-starvation, and loss of 15% or more of body weight

Antidiuretic hormone (ADH)   A hormone secreted by the pituitary gland that increases the amount of water reabsorbed by the kidneys

Antioxidant   A substance that is able to neutralize reactive molecules, reducing oxidative damage

Apparent temperature or **heat index**   A measure of how hot it feels when the relative humidity is added to the actual temperature

Atherosclerosis   A type of cardiovascular disease that involves the buildup of fatty material in artery walls

ATP (adenosine triphosphate)   The high-energy molecule used by the body to perform energy-requiring activities

Atrophy   A wasting away or decrease in size of a body part due to an abnormality, poor nutrition, or lack of use

Beta-hydroxy-beta-methylbutyrate (HMB)   A compound generated from the breakdown of the amino acid leucine; HMB is used by athletes as an ergogenic aid to reduce the muscle damage associated with intense physical effort.

Beta-oxidation   The breakdown of fatty acids into 2-carbon units that form acetyl-CoA

Bicarbonate   A compound present in the body that prevents changes in acidity; it is used as an ergogenic aid to neutralize lactic acid

Body mass index (BMI)   An index of weight in relation to height that is used to compare body size with a standard; BMI is equal to body weight (in kilograms) divided by height in meters squared.

Bulimia nervosa   An eating disorder characterized by a cycle of binging and purging

Calorie   Unit of heat that is used to express the amount of energy provided by foods; it is commonly used to refer to a kilocalorie, which is 1,000 calories.

Capillaries Small, thin-walled blood vessels in which gases and nutrients are exchanged between blood and cells

Carbohydrate loading or **glycogen supercompensation** A regimen of diet and exercise that is designed to load muscle glycogen stores beyond normal capacity

Cardiac muscle The type of muscle tissue that makes up the heart

Cardiac output The amount of blood pumped by the heart during a one-minute period

Carnitine A compound made from the amino acids lysine and methionine that is needed to transport fatty acids into the mitochondria; it is used as an ergogenic aid.

Cellular respiration The reactions that break down glucose, fatty acids, and amino acids in the presence of oxygen to produce carbon dioxide, water, and energy in the form of ATP.

Cholesterol A lipid made only by animal cells that consists of multiple chemical rings

Chromium picolinate A dietary supplement sold as an ergogenic aid; marketers claim that it will increase lean body mass and decrease body fat.

Citric acid cycle Also known as the Krebs cycle or the tricarboxylic acid cycle, this is the stage of cellular respiration in which acetyl-CoA is broken down into two molecules of carbon dioxide.

Creatine A nitrogen-containing compound found in muscle, where it is used to make creatine phosphate; it is used as an ergogenic aid to increase short-duration, high-power performance and increase muscle mass.

Creatine phosphate A high-energy compound found in muscle that can be broken down to form ATP

Dehydration A reduction in the amount of body water

Diabetes Also known as diabetes mellitus; a disease of carbohydrate metabolism caused by either insufficient insulin production or decreased sensitivity of cells to insulin. It results in elevated blood glucose levels.

Dietary references intakes (DRIs) A set of reference values for the intake of energy, nutrients, and food components that are used for planning and assessing the diets of healthy people in the United States and Canada

Electrolytes   Positively and negatively charged ions that conduct an electrical current in solution; the term commonly refers to sodium, potassium, and chloride.

Electron transport chain   The final stage of cellular respiration in which electrons are passed down a chain of molecules to oxygen, forming water and producing ATP

Energy balance   The amount of energy consumed in the diet compared with the amount expended by the body over a given period

Endorphins   Compounds that cause a natural euphoria and reduce the perception of pain under certain stressful conditions; endorphins may be the cause of the euphoria known as runner's high.

Energy-yielding nutrients   Nutrients, including carbohydrates, fats, and proteins, that can be metabolized to provide energy in the body

Enzymes   Protein molecules that accelerate the rate of chemical reactions in the body but are not altered by the reactions

Ephedra   A naturally occurring substance derived from the Chinese herb Ma huang; ephedra acts as a stimulant, increasing blood pressure and heart rate.

Ephedrine   The active ingredient in ephedra

Ergogenic aids   Substances that can enhance athletic performance

Erythropoietin (EPO)   A peptide hormone that stimulates stem cells in the bone marrow to differentiate into red blood cells; it is used as an ergogenic aid to increase endurance.

Essential nutrients   Nutrients that must be provided in the diet because the body either cannot make them or cannot make them in sufficient quantities to satisfy its needs

Estimated average requirements (EARs)   Intakes that meet the estimated nutrient needs (as defined by a specific indicator of adequacy) of 50% of people in a gender and life-stage group

Estimated energy requirements (EERs)   Recommendations for energy needs that are based on the amount of energy predicted to maintain energy balance in a healthy person of a defined age, gender, height, weight, and level of physical activity

Extracellular fluid   The fluid located outside cells; it includes fluid found in the blood, lymph, gastrointestinal tract, spinal column, eyes, and joints, and that found between cells and tissues.

Fast-twitch muscle fibers   Muscle cells that can contract very quickly and have a great capacity for ATP production via anaerobic metabolism

Fatigue   Being tired

Fatty acids   Lipids made up of chains of carbons linked to hydrogens with an acid group at one end

Female athlete triad   A syndrome in young female athletes that involves disordered eating, amenorrhea, and low bone density

Fiber   Substances, most of which are carbohydrates, that cannot be broken down by human digestive enzymes

Fortification   Adding nutrients to foods, such as vitamin D to milk

Free radicals   Atoms or molecules with one or more unpaired electrons; free radicals are often created inside the body as the result of outside pollutants (such as smoke) and can cause severe damage to body cells.

Ginseng   An herbal supplement promoted to increase endurance

Gluconeogenesis   The synthesis of glucose from simple noncarbohydrate molecules; amino acids from protein are the primary source of carbons for glucose synthesis.

Glucose   A monosaccharide that is the primary form of carbohydrate used to provide energy in the body

Glycogen   A carbohydrate made of many glucose molecules linked together in a highly branched structure; it is the storage form of carbohydrate in animals.

Glycolysis   A metabolic pathway in the cytoplasm of the cell that splits glucose into two 3-carbon molecules; the energy released from one molecule of glucose is used to make two ATP molecules.

Growth hormone   A peptide hormone produced by the pituitary gland that is important for growth and maintenance of lean tissue

Heat exhaustion   Low blood pressure, rapid pulse, fainting, and sweating caused when dehydration decreases blood volume so much that blood can no longer both cool the body and provide oxygen to the muscles

Heatstroke   Elevated body temperature as a result of fluid loss and the failure of the temperature regulatory center of the brain

Heat-related illness   Conditions, such as heat cramps, heat exhaustion, and heatstroke, that can occur due to an unfavorable combination of exercise, hydration status, and climatic conditions

Homeostasis   A physiological state in which a stable internal environment is maintained

Hormone   A chemical messenger that is secreted into the blood by one tissue and acts on cells in another part of the body

Hypertension   High blood pressure; defined as a blood pressure that is consistently elevated to 140/90 mm of mercury or greater

Hypertrophy   Enlargement or overgrowth of tissue

Hyponatremia   A low concentration of sodium in the blood

Interstitial fluid   The portion of the extracellular fluid located in the spaces between cells and tissues

Intracellular fluid   The fluid located inside cells

Ketones   Molecules formed when there is not sufficient carbohydrates to completely metabolize the acetyl-CoA produced from fat breakdown

Kilocalorie   See *Calorie.*

Kilojoule   A measure of work that can be used to express energy intake and energy output; 4.18 kjoules = 1 kcalorie

Lactic acid   An acid produced as an end product of anaerobic metabolism

Malnutrition   Any condition resulting from an energy or nutrient intake either above or below that which is optimal

Maximal oxygen consumption   See *Aerobic capacity.*

Medium chain triglycerides (MCTs) Fats containing fatty acids that have 8 to 10 carbons in their carbon chain; these fatty acids can be absorbed directly into the blood and do not require carnitine for transport into the mitochondria.

Metabolism The sum of all the chemical reactions that take place within a living organism

Myofibril Rodlike structures inside muscle cells that are responsible for muscle contraction

Myosin The contractile protein that makes up the thick filaments of muscle fibers

Nutrient density A measure of the nutrients provided by a food relative to the energy it contains

Nutrients Chemical substances in foods that provide energy, structure, and regulation for body processes

Nutrition A science that studies the interactions that occur between living organisms and food

Osmosis The movement of water across a membrane in a direction that will equalize the concentration of dissolved substances on each side

Osteoporosis A bone disorder characterized by a reduction in bone mass, increased bone fragility, and an increased risk of fractures

Overnutrition Poor nutritional status resulting from eating too much

Overtraining syndrome A collection of emotional, behavioral, and physical symptoms caused by training without enough rest to allow for recovery

PA (physical activity) value A numeric value associated with activity level that is a variable in the EER equations used to calculate energy needs

Phytochemical A substance found in plant foods that is not an essential nutrient, but may have health-promoting properties

Plasma The liquid portion of the blood that remains when the blood cells are removed

Prebiotics   Substances that pass undigested into the colon and stimulate the growth and/or activity of certain types of bacteria

Probiotics   Products that contain live bacteria; when probiotics are consumed, the bacteria live temporarily in the colon and confer health benefits.

Pyruvate   A 3-carbon molecule produced when glucose is broken down by glycolysis

Recommended dietary allowances (RDAs)   A recommended intake that is sufficient to meet the nutrient needs of almost all healthy people in a specific life-stage and gender group

Renin   An enzyme released by the kidneys when blood pressure drops. Renin helps to produce angiotensin II

Resting heart rate   The number of times that the heart beats per minute while a person is at rest

Ribose   A sugar that is needed to synthesize RNA and ATP

Saturated fats   Triglycerides containing fatty acids, with no carbon-carbon double bonds

Skeletal muscles   Muscles attached to the skeleton that are under voluntary control

Slow-twitch muscle fibers   Muscle cells that can continue to contract for long periods and rely primarily on aerobic metabolism

Smooth muscle   A type of muscle that is not under voluntary control; it lines blood vessels, air passageways, and the walls of glands and other organs.

Starch   A carbohydrate made of many glucose molecules linked in straight or branching chains; the bonds that hold the glucose molecules together can be broken by the human digestive enzymes.

Stroke volume   The amount of blood pumped by the heart with each beat

Tolerable Upper Intake Level (UL)   The maximum daily intake that is unlikely to pose risks of adverse health effects to most people in the specified life-stage and gender group

Trans fat   Triglycerides containing unsaturated fatty acids in which the hydrogen atoms are on opposite sides of the double bond

Triglycerides   A fat made of three fatty acids attached to a molecule of glycerol

Unsaturated fats   Triglycerides containing fatty acids with one or more carbon-carbon double bonds

Urea   A nitrogen-containing waste product that is excreted in the urine

VO$_2$max   See *Aerobic capacity.*

BIBLIOGRAPHY

Ament W. and G.J. Verkerke. "Exercise and Fatigue." *Sports Medicine.* 39:389-422, 2009.

American Dietetic Association. "Position of the American Dietetic Association: Weight Management." *Journal of the American Dietetic Association.* 109: 330-346, 2009.

Bahrke M.S., W.P. Morgan, and A. Stegner. "Is Ginseng an Ergogenic Aid?" *International Journal of Sport Nutrition and Exercise Metabolism.* 19:298-322, 2009.

Bemben, M.G. and H.S. Lamont. "Creatine Supplementation and Exercise Performance." *Sports Medicine.* 35:107-125, 2005.

Bent, S., T.N. Tiedt, M.C. Odden, and M.G. Shlipak. "The Relative Safety of Ephedra Compared with Other Herbal Products." *Annals of Internal Medicine.* 138: 468–471, 2003.

Berardi, J.M., T.B. Price, E.E. Noreen, and P.W. Lemon. "Postexercise Muscle Glycogen Recovery Enhanced with a Carbohydrate-Protein Supplement." *Medicine and Science in Sports and Exercise.* 38:1106–1113, 2006.

Birkeland, K.I., J. Stray-Gundersen, P. Hemmersbach, et al. "Effect of rhEPO Administration on Serum Levels of sTfR and Cycling performance." *Medicine and Science in Sports and Exercise.* 32:1238–1243, 2000.

Brass, E.P. "Carnitine and Sports Medicine: Use or Abuse?" *Annals of the New York Academy of Sciences.* 1033:67–78, 2004.

Brown, G.A., M. Vukovich, and D.S. King. "Testosterone Prohormone Supplements." *Medicine and Science in Sports and Exercise.* 38:1451–1461, 2006.

Bucci, L.R. "Selected Herbals and Human Exercise Performance." *American Journal of Clinical Nutrition.* 72: 624S–636S, 2000.

Bussar, V.A., T.J. Fairchild, A. Rao, et al. "Carbohydrate Loading in Human Muscle: An Improved One Day Protocol." *European Journal of Applied Physiology*. 87:290–295, 2002.

Centers for Disease Control and Prevention. "Diabetes Fact Sheet: General information and national estimates on diabetes in the United States, 2007." Available online at http://www.cdc.gov/diabetes/pubs/factsheet07.htm Accessed September 12, 2009.

Centers for Disease Control and Prevention. "Obesity and Overweight, Health Consequences." Available online at http://www.cdc.gov/obesity/causes/health.html Accessed September 12, 2009.

Centers for Disease Control and Prevention. "Physical Activity and Health: A Report of the Surgeon General." Available online at http://www.cdc.gov/nccdphp/sgr/adults.htm. Accessed March 9, 2010.

Centers for Disease Control and Prevention. "Prevalence of Overweight and Obesity Among Adults: United States 1999–2000." Available online at http://www.cdc.gov/nchs/releases/02news/obesityonrise.htm. Accessed October 12, 2009.

Centers for Disease Control and Prevention. "Trends in intake of energy and macronutrients – United States, 1971–2000." *Morbidity and Mortality Weekly Report*. 53:80–82, 2004.

Coon, K.A. and K.L. Tucker. "Television and Children's Consumption Patterns: A review of the literature." *Minerva Pediatrica* 54:423–436, 2002.

Costill, D.L., R. Thomas, R.A. Robergs, et al. "Adaptations to Swimming Training: Influence of Training Volume." *Medicine and Science in Sports and Exercise*. 23: 371–377, 1991.

Di Luigi, L. "Supplements and the Endocrine System in Athletes." *Clinical Sports Medicine*. 27:131–151, 2008.

Di Santolo, M., G. Stel, G. Banfi, et al. "Anemia and iron status in young fertile non-professional female athletes." *European Journal of Applied Physiology*. 102:703–709, 2008.

Douroudos, I.I., I.G. Fatouros, V. Gourgoulis, et al. "Dose-related Effects of Prolonged NaHCO3 Ingestion During High-intensity Exercise." *Medicine and Science in Sports and Exercise*. 38:1746-1753, 2006

Finaud, J., G. Lac, and E. Filaire. "Oxidative Stress: Relationship with Exercise and Training." *Sports Medicine*. 36:327–358, 2006.

Fontaine, K.R. "Physical Activity Improves Mental Health." Available online at http://www.physsportsmed.com/index.php?art=psm_10_2000?article=1256.

Gallagher, D., S. Heymsfield, M. Heo, et al. "Healthy Percentage Body Fat Ranges: An approach for developing guidelines based on body mass index." *American Journal of Clinical Nutrition*. 72:694–701, 2000.

Gill, H. and J. Prasad. "Probiotics, Immunomodulation, and Health Benefits." *Advances in Experimental Medicine and Biology*. 606:423–454, 2008.

Hill, J.O. and Wyatt, H.R. "Role of Physical Activity in Preventing and Treating Obesity." *Journal of Applied Physiology*. 99:765-70, 2005

Institute of Medicine, Food, and Nutrition Board, Institute of Medicine. "Dietary Reference Intakes: Vitamin A, Vitamin K, Arsenic, Boron, Chromium, Copper, Iodine, Iron, Manganese, Molybdenum, Nickel, Silicon, Vanadium, and Zinc." Washington, D.C.: National Academies Press, 2001.

Institute of Medicine, Food, and Nutrition Board. "Dietary Reference Intakes for Water, Potassium, Sodium, Chloride, and Sulfate." Washington, D.C.: National Academies Press, 2004.

Institute of Medicine, Food, and Nutrition Board. "Dietary Reference Intakes for Energy, Carbohydrates, Fiber, Fat, Protein, and Amino Acids." Washington, DC: National Academies Press, 2002.

Jackson, M.J., M. Khassaf, F. Vasilaki, et al. "Vitamin E and the Oxidative Stress of Exercise." *Annals of the New York Academy of Sciences*. 1031:158–168, 2004.

Jeukendrup, A.E. and S. Aldred. "Fat Supplementation, Health, and Endurance Performance." *Nutrition*. 20:678–688, 2004.

Kanaley, J.A. "Growth Hormone, Arginine, and Exercise." *Current Opinion in Clinical Nutrition and Metabolic Care*. 11:50-54, 2008.

Key, T. J., N.E. Allen, E.A. Spencer, and R.C. Travis. "The Effect of Diet on Risk of Cancer." *The Lancet*. 360 861–868, 2002.

Kraemer, W.J., D.L. Hatfield, J.S. Volek, et al. "Effects of Amino Acids Supplement on Physiological Adaptations to Resistance Training." *Medicine and Science in Sports and Exercise.* 41:1111-1121, 2009.

Kreider, R.B., C. Melton, M. Greenwood, et al. "Effects of Oral d-ribose Supplementation on Anaerobic Capacity and Selected Metabolic Markers in Healthy Males." *International Journal of Sport Nutrition and Exercise Metabolism.* 13: 87–96, 2003.

Liu, H., D.M. Bravata, I. Olkin, et al. "Systematic Review: The effects of growth hormone on athletic performance." *Annals of Internal Medicine.* 148:747–758, 2008.

Manore, M. and J. Thompson. *Sport Nutrition for Health and Performance.* Champaign, Ill.: Human Kinetics, 2000.

Manore, M.L., L.C. Kam, and A.B. Loucks. "The Female Athlete Triad: Components, nutrition issues, and health consequences." *Journal of Sports Sciences.* 25:S61-S71, 2007.

Margaritis, I. and A.S. Rousseau. "Does Physical Exercise Modify Antioxidant Requirements?" *Nutrition Research Reviews.* 21:3–12, 2008.

McArdle, W.D., F.I. Katch, and V.L. Katch. *Exercise Physiology: Energy, Nutrition, and Human Performance, 5th ed.* Baltimore: Lippincott Williams & Wilkins, 2002.

Misell, L.M., N.D. Lagomarcino, V. Schuster, and M. Kern. "Chronic Medium-chain Triacylglycerol Consumption and Endurance Performance in Trained Runners." *Journal of Sports Medicine and Physical Fitness.* 41: 210–215, 2001.

Montana State University, Bozeman. "Physiology and Psychology Performance Benchmarks." Available online at

http://btc.montana.edu/olympics/physiology/pb02.html. Accessed December 27, 2009.

National Center for Health Statistics. "Health United States, 2008." Available online at http://www.cdc.gov/nchs/data/hus/hus08.pdf#070. Accessed September 11, 2009.

Nissen, S.L. and R.L. Sharp. "Effect of Dietary Supplements on Lean Mass and Strength Gains with Resistance Exercise: A meta-analysis." *Journal of Applied Physiology.* 94:651–659, 2003.

National Oceanic and Atmospheric Administration. "National Weather Service: Heat Index." Available online at http://www.weather.gov/os/heat/index.shtml. Accessed March 10, 2009.

NutraBio.com. "Congress Passes Steroid Control Act." Available online at http://www.nutrabio.com/News/news.steroid_control_act_2.htm. Accessed June 25, 2008.

O'Connor, D.M. and M.J. Crowe. "Effects of Six Weeks of Beta-hydroxy-beta-methylbutyrate (HMB) and HMB/creatine Supplementation on Strength, Power, and Anthropometry of Highly Trained Athletes." *Journal of Strength and Conditioning Research* 21:419–423, 2007.

Op't Eijnde, B., M. Van Leemputte, F. Brouns, et al. "No Effects of Oral Ribose Supplementation on Repeated Maximal Exercise and De Novo ATP Resynthesis." *Journal of Applied Physiology.* 91: 2275–2281, 2002.

Paddon-Jones, D., E. Borsheim, R.R. Wolfe. "Potential Ergogenic Effects of Arginine and Creatine Supplementation." *Journal of Nutrition.* 134:2888S–2894S, 2004.

Pearce, P. Z. "A Practical Approach to the Overtraining Syndrome." *Current Sports Medicine Reports.* 1:179–183, 2002.

Raymer, G.H., G.D. Marsh, J.M. Kowalchuk, and R.T. Thompson. "Metabolic Effects of Induced Alkalosis During Progressive Forearm Exercise to Fatigue." *Journal of Applied Physiology.* 96:2050–2056, 2004.

Remick, D., K. Chancellor, J. Pederson, et al. "Hyperthermia and dehydration-related deaths associated with intentional rapid weight loss in three collegiate wrestlers—North Carolina, Wisconsin, and Michigan, November–December, 1997." *Morbidity and Mortality Weekly Report.* 47:105–108, 1997. Available online at http://www.cdc.gov/mmwr/preview/mmwrhtml/00051388.htm. Accessed March 25, 2009.

Ritter, S.K. "Faster, Higher, Stronger." *Chemical Engineering News.* 77: 42–52, 1999.

Rodriguez, N.R., N.M. DiMarco, and S. Langley. "Position of the American Dietetic Association, Dietitians of Canada, and the American College of Sports Medicine: Nutrition and athletic performance." *Journal of the American Dietetic Association.* 109:509-527, 2009.

Shao, A. and J.N. Hathcock. "Risk Assessment for Creatine Monohydrate." *Regulatory Toxicology and Pharmacology.* 45:242–251, 2006.

Sökmen, B., L.E. Armstrong, W.J. Kraemer, et al. "Caffeine Use in Sports: Considerations for the Athlete." *Journal of Strength and Conditioning Research.* 22:978–986, 2008.

Suedekum, N.A. R.J. and Dimeff. "Iron and the Athlete." *Current Sports Medicine Report.* 4:199–202, 2005.

Tokish, J.M., M.S. Kocher, and R.J. Hawkins. "Ergogenic Aids: A Review of Basic Science, Performance, Side Effects, and Status in Sports." *American Journal of Sports Medicine.* 32:1543–1553, 2004.

U.S. Department of Health and Human Services, U.S. Department of Agriculture. "Dietary Guidelines for Americans, 2005." Available online at http://www.healthierus.gov/dietaryguidelines.

U.S. Department of Health and Human Services. "2008 Physical Activity Guidelines for Americans." Washington, D.C.: Department of Health and Human Services, 2008.

U.S. Food and Drug Administration. "Evidence Report/Technology Assessment Number 76. Ephedra and Ephedrine for Weight Loss and Athletic Performance Enhancement: Clinical Efficacy and Side Effects." Available online at http://www.fda.gov/bbs/topics/NEWS/ephedra/summary.html.

U.S. Food and Drug Administration. FDA White Paper. "Health Effects of Androsteinedione." March 11, 2004. Available online at http://www.fda.gov/oc/whitepapers/andro.html.

Wilson G.J., J.M. Wilson, and A.H. Manninen. "Effects of beta-hydroxy-beta-methylbutyrate (HMB) on exercise performance and body composition across varying levels of age, sex, and training experience: A review." *Nutrition and Metabolism (Lond).* 5:1-8, 2008.

FURTHER RESOURCES

American College of Sports Medicine and the American Heart Association Physical Activity and Public Health. "Updated Recommendation for Adults: Updated Recommendations for Medical Science Sports and Exercise," Vol. 39, No. 8, pp. 1423–1434, 2007.

Duyff, Roberta. *American Dietetic Association Complete Food and Nutrition Guide.* 3rd ed. CITY, John Wiley & Sons. 2008.

NIH Office of Dietary Supplements. "Dietary Supplement Fact Sheets." Available online at http://dietarysupplements.info.nih.gov/Health_Information/Information_About_Individual_Dietary_Supplements.aspx.

U.S. Department of Health and Human Services. *A Healthier You: Based on the Dietary Guidelines for Americans.* Office of Disease Prevention and Health Promotion U.S., 2005.

U.S. Department of Health and Human Services. "Be Active Your Way: A Guide for Adults." Available online at http://www.health.gov/paguidelines/adultguide/default.aspx.

Web Sites
President's Council on Physical Fitness and Sports
http://www.fitness.gov

This site provides the latest guidelines for physical fitness for Americans. It also includes information on how to start a physical activity program today and stay active and fit for life.

WE CAN
http://www.nhlbi.nih.gov/health/public/heart/obesity/wecan/

We Can! *stands for Ways to Enhance Children's Activity & Nutrition.* We Can! *is a national education program designed for parents and caregivers to help children 8-13 years old stay at a healthy weight.* We Can! *offers parents and families tips and fun activities to encourage healthy eating, increase physical activity, and reduce sedentary or screen time.*

Physical Activity Guidelines for Americans: US Department of Human Services
http://www.health.gov/paguidelines/guidelines/default.aspx
This site provides access to the government guidance to help Americans improve their health through appropriate physical activity.

HealthFinder.gov
http://www.healthfinder.gov/
This site provides a guide to reliable information on physical activity and other health issues.

PICTURE CREDITS

INDEX

Page numbers in *italics* indicate photos or illustrations; page numbers followed by *t* indicate tables.

ABOUT THE AUTHORS

LORI A. SMOLIN, PH.D., received her B.S. degree from Cornell University, where she studied human nutrition and food science. She received her doctorate from the University of Wisconsin at Madison. Her doctoral research focused on B vitamins, homocysteine accumulation, and genetic defects in homocysteine metabolism. She completed postdoctoral training both at the Harbor–UCLA Medical Center, where she studied human obesity, and at the University of California at San Diego, where she studied genetic defects in amino acid metabolism. She has published in these areas in peer-reviewed journals. She and Mary Grosvenor are coauthors of several well-respected college-level nutrition textbooks and contributing authors for a middle school text. Dr. Smolin is currently at the University of Connecticut, where she teaches in the Department of Nutritional Science. Courses she has taught include introductory nutrition, life-cycle nutrition, food preparation, nutritional biochemistry, general biochemistry, and introductory biology.

MARY B. GROSVENOR, M.S., R.D., received her B.A. degree in English from Georgetown University and her M.S. in nutrition sciences from the University of California at Davis. She is a registered dietitian (R.D.) with experience in public health, clinical nutrition, and nutrition research. She has published in peer-reviewed journals in the areas of nutrition and cancer and methods of assessing dietary intake. She and Lori Smolin are the coauthors of several well-respected college-level nutrition textbooks and contributing authors of a middle school text. Grosvenor has taught introductory nutrition to community college and nursing school students. In addition to writing and teaching, she counsels patients as a hospital dietitian and certified diabetes educator and advises other health professionals in the area of clinical nutrition.